UNLOCKING STUDENT TALENT

THE NEW SCIENCE OF DEVELOPING EXPERTISE

ROBIN J. FOGARTY / GENE M. KERNS / BRIAN M. PETE

FOREWORD BY K. ANDERS ERICSSON AND ROBERT POOL

TEACHERS COLLEGE PRESS

TEACHERS COLLEGE | COLUMBIA UNIVERSITY

NEW YORK AND LONDON

Published by Teachers College Press, 1234 Amsterdam Avenue, New York, NY 10027

Cover design by David K. Kessler. Photo by Vizerskaya, Getty Images.

Library of Congress Cataloging-in-Publication Data

Names: Fogarty, Robin, author. | Kerns, Gene M., author. | Pete, Brian M., author.
Title: Unlocking student talent : the new science of developing expertise / Robin J. Fogarty, Gene M. Kerns, Brian M. Pete foreword by Anders Ericsson and Robert Pool.
Description: New York, NY : Teachers College Press, [2018] | Includes bibliographical references and index.
Identifiers: LCCN 2017039811| ISBN 9780807758724 (pbk. : acid-free paper ISBN 9780807776674 (ebook)
Subjects: LCSH: Learning ability. | Personality and intelligence. | Personality and academic achievement. | Cognitive styles.
Classification: LCC LB1134 .F65 2018 | DDC 370.15/23—dc23
LC record available at https://lccn.loc.gov/2017039811

ISBN 978-0-8077-5872-4 (paper)
ISBN 978-0-8077-7667-4 (ebook)

Printed on acid-free paper
Manufactured in the United States of America

25 24 23 22 21 20 19 18   8 7 6 5 4 3 2 1

In memory of my mother, Margaret Peery Kerns Locks,
who was my greatest teacher.
—Gene M. Kerns

In admiration of our nephew, Brian Preston Pete,
for his belief and adherence to thousands of hours of practice to perfect
his golf game—just like he remembers his Dad, Kevin Pete, doing.
—Brian M. Pete and Robin J. Fogarty

Contents

Foreword

During the last decade, we have seen compelling evidence that individuals can achieve high levels of performance through extended training. In particular more than two dozen books have been published, describing detailed studies of the specific types of training that expert performers had engaged in during their childhood and adolescence and discussing how this knowledge can help individuals improve their own performance. The focus of most of these books—several of them bestsellers—has been on how world-class performers were able, through practice, to attain levels of achievement that have traditionally been assumed to require innate gifts and superior genes. With this growing understanding of the developmental path of expert performers in many different domains, our next task is to make that knowledge available to all motivated individuals, allowing them to take their own performance to new levels. Perhaps the most important question facing our society is how these findings and insights can be used to improve and redesign general education and help classroom teachers encourage students to develop into independent learners and skilled performers.

It is this important question that Robin Fogarty, Gene Kerns, and Brian Pete address in their new book. In our opinion, the three have done an outstanding job of extracting the relevant information from the massive collection of books that have been published on the topic. Perhaps the most impressive aspect of this new book is how it organizes and integrates information from authors that write from diverse theoretical perspectives.

The book has three major sections. In the first, the authors discuss how to get students engaged and interested in learning in school, and they handle this challenging topic particularly well. Teachers in the general education system are at a disadvantage here when compared with sports coaches and teachers of music or dance, whose charges have generally chosen to participate in these activities and presumably had some initial interest. By contrast, a classroom teacher must help every child improve their performance and start building skills, no matter how little motivation they may have or what abilities they may bring to the classroom. Another disadvantage that general education teachers face is that they typically deal with a much larger number of students (typically 20–25) in their classrooms. Teachers in other domains may encounter more favorable student-to-teacher ratios, with a smaller group of students per adult teacher, and sometimes even one-on-one instruction. Fogarty, Kerns, and Pete do a remarkable job assembling evidence and insights on how teachers can inspire students and instill knowledge in classrooms.

The second section of this book lays out a vision for how different kinds of effective training and practice observed in many other domains of activity can transform general education and help students improve their performance and build skills. The authors describe methods that have proven successful in developing learning environments, where students actively engage in classroom activities and perform repeated tasks with immediate feedback and with the goal of changing behavior and building skills. More traditional education has tended to offer students opportunities to learn and then interpreted students' failures as due to a lack of innate cognitive capacities. New insights into the structure of acquired skills provide deep insights into how guided instruction and designed practice can help initially struggling students gradually increase their performance and reach educational goals.

The third section of the book is, in our view, the most exciting, as it discusses the prospect of developing students as increasingly independent learners, as commonly viewed in other domains such as music or chess. The goal is to follow the pattern seen in these other domains, with the students gradually developing the skills they need to take over the role of their teachers, so that by the time they graduate they are able to think and reason independently. Ideally, students should be able to evaluate their own and others' arguments and performance in at least a couple of domains of expertise. They should be able to plan for and anticipate actions in real-world situations and then successfully reflect on outcomes and identify corrective actions or areas in which they need additional practice.

This book offers revolutionary proposals for transforming general education and, in particular, describes how to produce high-school graduates who are independent learners prepared and ready to employ the appropriate methods in acquiring whatever skills they need to succeed in their careers. Given today's rapidly changing technological environment, our school system must develop and train graduates in such a way that they are equipped to continue development of their performance throughout their adult years—years that can be expected to include multiple transitions to new careers, and many of which will require skills as entrepreneurs and self-employed agents. In short, it is time to start modifying the current education system to match the demands of the third millennium. This book is an excellent place to start.

—*K. Anders Ericsson and Robert Pool*

Preface

Unlocking student talent is about transforming students with the "reachfulness code" that begins by igniting motivation; grows with deep, deliberate practice, and is supported to the highest levels by master coaching. This book celebrates the many instances of unlocking talent in our schools, homes, neighborhoods, and communities. In fact, there are unknown numbers of kids who go through the motions of education, schooling, or whatever learning opportunities are available to them, yet never really buy into or get hooked by an undiscovered or undisclosed passion for learning something, whatever that something might be.

Still, when teachers/coaches observe both their eager and their reluctant students, they hope that their teaching will unlock a desire to learn, develop a hidden talent or potential or even a burning desire within the student, and herd these kids toward achievement. Teachers/coaches can light the fire within each one in their care. They can carve out and develop "deliberate practice" routines, and guide the youngsters with timely, specific, and productive coaching and individualized feedback. In return, talent flourishes, potential blossoms, and untapped skills explode with a grace and elegance unknown to so many.

Our hope is that with the theoretical grounding and explicit steps offered in this book, teachers can see this happen with more and more of their students. By being talent nurturers in classrooms or gyms and by applying these simple, researched techniques designed for our teaching/coaching communities, teachers hold the reins for the force of power called the "talent code."

Insightful, inspiring, and well-intentioned teacher/coaches and mentors are in positions of great, if sometimes invisible, influence, and their impact cannot be underestimated. Talent, potential, skill, and the gifts of athleticism, academic acumen, elegance and grace in the performing arts, or the magical transformations of the culinary arts, engineering, and design yield results when these master teacher/coaches work their wonders and develop talent and potential beyond our wildest imaginations. The results they attain with these youngsters of "talent (potential) yet to be tapped," are far-reaching, standout performances that break records every day, earn awards and accolades, and many times open students' eyes and inspire their dedication to an interest or passion that they then pursue to their great satisfaction over a lifetime.

We have divided our discussion of how to unlock student talent into three parts, each with three chapters.

OVERVIEW: PARTS AND CHAPTERS

Part I. Motivating: Spark the Passion: Initiate, maintain, and sustain the learner's motivation.

Chapter 1. Inspire: Inspiration consists of the spark that generates motivation. It is connected to four particular catalysts: aspirations, hallmarks, competiveness, and novelty.

Chapter 2. Invigorate: Invigorating motivation as an ongoing driver, the following markers are highlighted: challenge, competiveness, hallmarks, and creativity.

Chapter 3. Instill: Ideas that bear on instilling continuing motivation as an intrinsic attribute are discussed: mindset, confidence, will, passion, burning desire, and pride.

Part II. Practicing: Engineer to Develop Expertise: Learn practice and adopt the rigorous routines of reach and repeat practice iterations.

Chapter 4. The Repetitions: Learners witness the mystery and magic of myelin and its stunning relationship to practice that pays off.

Chapter 5. Resistance and Results: This is where teachers discuss the concept of "reachfulness" that empowers practice routines by working in a zone that is just out of reach.

Chapter 6. Recovery and Residual: Learners realize the cultivation of mental maps evolving from the right kind of routines, cultivated constantly, developing "pattern-thinking."

Part III. Coaching: Seek Extraordinary Excellence: Settle for nothing less than one's personal best.

Chapter 7. Engage: This is the phase when the coach and talent become a team, talking and conferring constantly on skill levels, as well as developing deliberate practice routines as a bond of trust develops.

Chapter 8. Elevate: The master coach elevates performance literally, deliberately, and strategically, to develop and hone the students' current performance achievement through reachfulness.

Chapter 9. Exceed: Exceeding the standard or the current skill level has the master coach moving the students beyond the original goals through goal setting, imagination, and metacognitive reflection.

Part III Classroom Teaching Ideas: Circling back to the message of the book, which is clear, concise, and timely as we heighten the experience of the children in our care, we focus om how to unlock student talent with the "reachfulness code" that begins by igniting motivation, grows with deep, deliberate practice, and is supported to the highest levels by master coaching.

It's our greatest challenge by far, yet the stage seems set for the success we anticipate.

Acknowledgments

Professional Voices

While there are many informed voices sprinkled throughout this text, our initial impetus for doing this book was sparked by an amazing, groundbreaking book, *The Talent Code*, by Daniel Coyle (2009). Coyle drew on the decades of work by Anders Ericsson and his many colleagues to bring fascinating research on expertise to a mass audience. While we were still reflecting on the implications of *The Talent Code*, Anders Ericsson and colleague Robert Pool synthesized earlier research and published a remarkable book: *Peak: Secrets from the New Science of Expertise* (2016b). One other contributor, Malcolm Gladwell (2008) was also instrumental in furthering awareness about the role of practice. He popularized the works of Ericsson and others with his summary of the research in *Outliers: The Story of Success,* where he coined the phrase "The 10,000 Hour Rule." While not exact enough—and warranting a serious response from Ericsson and Pool (2016a)—it still was the first appearance of this information for many in the public sector. In sum, all we could think about was, "What if these findings would work in schools?" And off we went. To these three inspirational authors we owe a huge debt of gratitude.

In addition, there were several others we must mention specifically. The groundbreaking work of Rick Stiggins, leading the field early with ideas about assessing for learning, and Dylan Wiliam's expanding works on formative assessment are threaded throughout our discussions. And we are forever thankful to Lemov, Woolway, and Yezzi (2012) for their remarkable wisdom when they said, "We believe our profession is on the brink of greatness." (p. xv). This is an idea whose time has come, and we have used their ideas generously.

Professional Colleagues

As with most robust endeavors, including writing a book, the authors did not work in a vacuum. Initial sharing of the seed of this idea, conversations digging into possibilities, opinions pro and con on a million little tweaks, big ideas offered, reading in quick time, editing on the run, rereading one more time, and a constant stream of encouraging words that kept the ball rolling are what these colleagues did for the three of us. To Jan Bryan, Jean Ward, Ivette Gonzales, Julie Constanzo, Polly Everette, Jan Bryan, Cheryl Ballou, and, of course, our longtime colleague, Jim Bellanca, we are vastly appreciative of your time, energy, and genuine interest in our project, and we are truly indebted to you for your willingness to listen, mostly, but also to do whatever we needed at the moment to get to the next step. Thank you all.

Publishing Professionals

Foundational to the publication of the actual product, there are many hands that touch the manuscript, from inception to completion. These are the people who have developed their expertise in the various areas of acquiring, signing, shaping, writing, editing, reviewing, designing, proofing, and indexing the manuscript. In particular, we feel so fortunate that we have the editor-extraordinaire in our corner. Jean Ward was on board instantly when we approached her, and she shepherded our author team through the initial blast of ideas that spewed like a volcano, trimming our initial ideas in the first draft, and leading us all the way to the final book. For all her generous and timely assistance and leadership, we thank her. With that said, we know there are many individuals, whose names we don't even know, who made our ideas come to fruition in this brand new publication that we can't wait to share with our schools. A huge thank you to each and every person who had a critical part in producing one of our favorite things as educators—a new book to read.

Introduction

What do we know about the science of expertise? It is expected that mechanics understand every part of a car and how it all works together. Chefs must know each ingredient and the best cooking techniques. Architects must know every angle and surface. Yet, as "architects of the intellect," do we educators have a deep understanding of how expertise is developed? Can we align our daily work most appropriately with the process of developing expertise and excellence? Ultimately, a primary goal of teaching is to build and foster expertise and the desire for it in our students. Despite this noble goal, however, we cannot always be aware of recent research advances in this emerging field of how expertise is developed.

THE PURPOSE

The purpose of this work is to look at the research on world-class performance, with the particular goal of distilling it for educators and applying it in classrooms. Armed with the insights this research can offer, educators will be on the brink of new achievements.

The first step is to fully realize the breadth of potential that exists. As Ericsson and colleagues emphasize, we need to "forget the folklore about genius that makes many people think they cannot take a scientific approach to developing expertise" (Ericsson, Prietula, & Cokely, 2007, p. 116). Teachers can promote expertise systematically and consistently, and research documents this. Because of the importance of the science of expertise, it seems prudent for all stakeholders in the educational arena—school leaders, teachers, and students who are on the brink of greatness—to know the true story of expertise.

World-class performance is the subject of many stories. It makes for great fiction. "Popular lore is full of stories about unknown athletes, writers, and artists who become famous overnight, seemingly because of innate talent—they're 'naturals' people say" (Ericsson, Prietula, & Cokely, 2007, p. 119). The problem is that the way greatness is depicted is most often completely fictitious. Hollywood fuels the idea of individuals who are "naturals," but the science tells us this is not the case.

The study of how expertise develops it not new. One of the first writers to explore the topic was English aristocrat Sir Francis Galton, whose major works were published first in the mid-19th century and, amazingly, remain in print today. Though his name may not be familiar, we immediately recognize a phrase he coined: "nature versus nurture." In fact, Galton's views on expertise represented a struggle between these two influences. As a young man, Galton believed that people were born with roughly the same capacities, which then may, or may not, be developed over life, and that a great portion of human potential was untapped.

However, Galton changed his perspective on things when he read the writings of his eminently famous cousin, Charles Darwin. Swayed by the case for heredity and natural selection, Galton (1869/2006) later wrote, "I have no patience with the hypothesis . . . that babies are born pretty much alike, and that the sole agencies in creating differences between boy and boy, man and man, are steady application and moral effort" (p. 56).

Yet within his view that heredity was very much dominant, Galton (1869/2006) did indirectly acknowledge additional factors in that his concept of natural ability contains three parts. One is clearly genetic. He refers to this as "capacity." But he also acknowledges that "eminence" is the result of capacity, "zeal," and "an adequate power of doing great work" (p. 39). Galton's works on the subject of expertise remained dominant until quite recently. This is witnessed by their continued publication and the continued discussions of "giftedness," which Galton began.

According to statistician David Banks (1997), if we view talent and expertise as natural occurrences randomly distributed throughout the world—as Galton did—then there is a "problem of excess genius." He asserted that "the most important question we can ask of historians is, 'Why are some periods and places so astonishingly more productive than the rest?'" In particular, he notes the following three places and times as ones of inexplicable genius, using historical views on innate ability: (1) Athens, from about 440 B.C.E. to 380 B.C.E.; (2) Florence, from about 1440 to 1490; and (3) London, from about 1570 to 1640. At the times listed, Athens was the pinnacle of the achievements in Ancient Greece; Florence was the epicenter of the Italian Renaissance, and the English literary scene of London included Shakespeare, Milton, Bacon, and Donne.

Banks (1997) feels that "it is intellectually embarrassing that [the question of why some periods are so astonishingly productive] is almost never posed squarely, although its answer would have thrilling implications for education, politics, science, and art." This answer to this essential question is at the core of research on expertise.

10,000 HOURS

The modern exploration of expertise consistently traces back to the work of Anders Ericsson and his colleagues. Far from Galton's heredity-based view, modern authors in the field proclaim, "Consistently and overwhelmingly, the evidence showed that experts are always made, not born" (Ericsson, Prietula, & Cokely, 2007, p. 116). After a substantial period of time in scholarly journals, the work of Ericsson

> "Consistently and overwhelmingly, the evidence showed that experts are always made, not born."

and his colleagues began to make it to the mainstream in works like *Outliers*, with Gladwell's (2008) simplified interpretation of Ericsson's studies, for which Gladwell coined the phrase "The 10,000 Hour Rule." Additional works drawing from the research base include *Talent Is Overrated* (Colvin, 2008) and *The Talent Code* (Coyle, 2009). Yet, with the exception of Lemov et al.'s (2012) exploration of practice in *Practice Perfect: 42 Rules for Getting Better at Getting Better*, no one has yet fully explored the direct implications of this research for educators.

One possible reason why educators have not seen immediate implications for this research is that many works have taken a case study approach, profiling individuals. This made generalizing their findings for broad application within schools difficult. Within the body of works on expertise, Dan Coyle took a very different approach, one much closer to schools. Instead of studying individuals, in *The Talent Code* Coyle (2009) chose to study "hotbeds of talent": towns, schools, and even entire countries, current or historical, that have consistently produced a wildly disproportionate number of highly talented individuals. Banks (1997) might call these "concentrations of excess genius."

Coyle's (2009) work asks, how does one explain the dominance of the Brontë sisters within Victorian literature? Charlotte, Emily, and Anne were successful authors. Any family would be happy having one child achieve literary success. The Brontës got three! Similarly, a tiny strip mall vocal school in Dallas has had its students go on to sign millions of dollars in recording contracts, and a seemingly modest music school in the Adirondacks lists among its former students some of the greatest living string instrumentalists: Itzhak Perlman, Yo-Yo Ma, and Joshua Bell. Saying that there must be "something in the water" is not scientifically adequate to explain this success. Determining what these places do differently illuminates the talent code, which Coyle (2009) says contains three elements: deep practice, ignition, and master coaching.

Ultimately, research consistently shows that our potential is not predestined or determined by our genes. "Talent is not a possession. It's a construction project and [educators] are the foremen" (Coyle, personal communication, 2011). As foremen of this critical process, we need to better understand its elements and procedures.

Forget Everything You Know

To dismiss what one thinks about expertise, down to the genetic level, involves changing deeply held beliefs. If we are to apply these new understandings about the science of expertise in our schools, two major thought changes must occur. First, we must dispel the myth of gene-based, predestined talent. Then, we must understand how talent develops through physiological changes in our brains.

Because of the widely held beliefs that talent and expertise are a result of genetic predisposition, a rethinking of some genetic basics is warranted. For most of us, the story of genetics began with the pea plant–growing Augustinian friar, Gregor Mendel, who pioneered study in this area. Armed with knowledge of dominant and recessive traits, we followed Mendel's lead, dutifully filling in our Punnet squares, applying what we thought was precise science to determine predictable genetic outcomes.

What we now know is that genes are far more complex and defy the simple logic of Punnet squares, which cannot always explain genetic outcomes. The problem with our Mendelian/Punnet Square–based perspective on genetics, where dominant and recessive determine outcomes, is that it only applies—and then not always—to a limited number of features. It doesn't take into account the fact that "genes are constantly activated and deactivated by environmental stimuli, nutrition, hormones, nerve impulses, and other genes" meaning that "the exact same gene can produce different [outcomes] depending on how and when it is activated" (Shenk, 2011, pp. 22, 24).

Admittedly, "there are many elementary physical traits like eye, hair, and skin color where the process is near Mendelian—where certain genes produce predictable outcomes most of the time," but "the more complex the trait, the farther any one gene is from direct[ly] impacting the eventual outcome" (Shenk, 2011, pp. 24, 26). Given that manifestations of talent and expertise are incredibly complex, attempting to predict the outcomes using extremely basic approaches is futile. We need a new model.

GxE Mindset

Ultimately, experts in the field suggest that we abandon our "nature versus nurture" and reference "genes plus environment" (G + E) perspectives in

favor of a "G × E" mindset, which attempts to capture the dynamic interaction (×) between genes (G)
and the environment (E) where neither holds the
trump card in determining how things will unfold.
Synonymous with this is the concept of "dynamic
development." According to Shenk (2011), "Dynamic development is the new paradigm for talent,
lifestyle, and well-being. It is how genes influence
everything but strictly determine very little" (p. 33).

> Ultimately, experts in the field suggest that we abandon our "nature versus nurture" and reference "genes plus environment." "Dynamic development is the new paradigm for talent, lifestyle, and well-being. It is how genes influence everything but strictly determine very little."

   The physical manifestation of dynamic development is seen in William Walter Greulich's 1957 study
comparing the height of Japanese children raised in
California with those raised in Japan. With the simi-
larity of a nearly identical gene pool and the environmental differences of better nutrition and medical
care in California at the time, the California-raised
children were an amazing 5 inches taller than their Japanese homeland coun-
terparts. Clearly, environment has a substantial impact.

   The second modern understanding about how talent and expertise are
developed relates to physiological changes in our brains that we are just now
beginning to fully understand. While many of us are familiar with the quint-
essential black cabs of London, few of us realize the intense, multiyear, and
brain-altering process that is required to earn the cabbie license and ultimately pass a rigorous test referred to as "The Knowledge," which covers all of
London's streets and major sites. The process, according to Rosen (2014)
"has been called the hardest test, of any kind, in the world. Its rigors have
been likened to those required to earn a degree in law or medicine. It is
without question a unique intellectual, psychological and physical ordeal, demanding unnumbered thousands of hours of immersive study, as would-be
cabbies undertake the task of committing to memory the entirety of London, and demonstrating that mastery through a progressively more difficult
sequence of oral examinations—a process which, on average, takes four years
to complete."

   Before and after studies have documented that at the end of the arduous
process, the newly certified "London taxi drivers had more gray matter [in
areas of their brain related to spatial understanding] than people who were
similar in age, education and intelligence, but who did not drive taxis" and
"the longer someone had been driving a taxi, the larger his hippocampus, as
though the brain expanded to accommodate the cognitive demands of nav-
igating London's streets" (Jabr, 2011). The hours of study and practice had
literally changed their brains.

Myelin Matters

Numerous discussions of expertise reference extensive hours of deliberate practice, and we will address this, but among the earliest to discuss the results of practice from a physiological perspective was Dan Coyle in *The Talent Code*, when he explored new insights about myelin, a white substance that surrounds the axons of some nerve cells. Coyle points out that while knowledge of myelin is not new to us, it was historically viewed as far more inert then we now understand it to be.

In the early years of brain-based learning, "neurons and synapses [got] the lion's share of research attention" (Coyle, 2009, p. 40). University of Illinois professor Bill Greenough remarked, "We'd been ignoring myelin; then, around 2000, new imaging technologies gave us the capacity to explore myelin like never before, and the findings were staggering. In study after study across multiple fields of expertise, the correlations between myelin and ability were unquestionable" (Greenough as quoted in Coyle, 2009, p. 29).

As Coyle (2009) notes, myelin provides us "a vivid new model" for understanding talent because how it grows is no longer a mystery: It grows through practice or repetition. Research done by Dr. R. Douglas Fields (National Institutes of Health) and others on how myelin grows is summarized by Coyle (2009) as follows:

> The more the nerve fires, the more myelin wraps around it. The more myelin wraps around it, the faster the signals travel, increasing velocities up to one hundred times over signals sent through an uninsulated fiber. (p. 40)

Metaphorically speaking, "Myelin quietly transforms narrow alleys into broad, lightning-fast super-highways" (Coyle, 2009, pp. 40–41). The increased transmission speed of a highly myelinated neural circuit coupled with the reduced "refractory time (wait time required between one signal and the next)" which also develops, "boost overall information-processing capability by 3,000 times" in contrast with an unmyelinated pathway (Coyle, 2009, p. 41). So, Serena Williams executes functions related to tennis with far more efficiency and precision than someone first picking up a tennis racket because the neural pathways of her brain have been altered substantially by practice. Yo-Yo Ma masterfully draws a bow across a cello's strings with precision unmatched by any novice cellist because practice has rewired his brain to be able to do so.

In short, genes do not predetermine talent and the development of expertise. From a physiological perspective it is really the building up of myelin through sustained practice, a process that literally changes our brains and increases our abilities exponentially.

So, if expertise is physiologically within most everyone's capacity, why do so few reach appreciable heights? To fully understand this, Coyle's talent code elements are useful. Beyond the myelin-building deep or deliberate practice, considerations of ignition or motivation are needed, as well as the input of a master coach. Without a motivational drive, doing the necessary deliberate practice is nearly impossible, and without a master coach to guide and inform the process, it is likely that practice will not be appropriately directed to extraordinary levels of excellence and expertise.

Our Journey

In this book, we will begin by exploring ignition or motivation, which can take two forms. One form of motivation is the slow stoking-of-the-fire kind, which we will consider in Part III. But sometimes ignition is a "big bang" of energy. It's the explosive moment when a student is so inspired by a performance that she decides that she would like to learn a specific skill or develop a specific ability. This is the focus of Part I.

We will then transition to exploring deliberate practice, which is the actual stuff of expertise making. We have the potential to become experts, but only through deliberate practice. Thus in Part II we will juxtapose deliberate practice with what most of us do when we merely practice, and discuss how we can bring more deliberate practice to our classrooms. To be clear, it is through deliberate practice that experts are made, but the quantity and rigors of such practice require us to also thoroughly explore motivation. As Barr (2012) puts it, most often "motivation becomes the real constraint on expertise."

In Part III we will turn our attention to master teaching or coaching for expertise. In this section, we will also be exploring the other form of ignition, the slow stoking-of-the-fire kind, which is so essential due to the thousands of hours of deliberate practice necessary for eminence.

The Mission

Teaching for expertise might seem daunting to some K–12 educators who possibly view their role as generalists, but studies clearly show that expertise traces back to early beginnings—the first time one ever touches a piano, picks up a paintbrush, or first makes sense of letters or numbers. The mission is clear. If educators want to take students to higher levels, if we are to prepare students for college and career-readiness, if the mission is to foster those "on the brink of greatness," understanding the true story of expertise can enable teachers to lay more effective foundations for student expertise to bud, blossom, and flower.

MOTIVATING:
Spark the Passion

To accomplish great things, we must not only act, but also dream; not only plan, but also believe.

—Anatole France

Focusing on the word pairs in the quotation, "act, but also dream; . . . plan, but also believe" seems a perfect way to illuminate the concepts of motivation, drive, and perseverance to form the context of Part I. Think how these three elements interact to create a truly inspired, invigorated talent, with the needed attitudes and dispositions instilled deeply within someone's innermost self.

Defining moments are inspired by self; by family and fame; by teacher, coach, mentor; by peers. Inspiration consists of motivation that more often than not sprouts from a piqued interest that percolates within the talent. It may be self-initiated by happenstance as youngsters move about their respective worlds, or perhaps it is introduced by someone else through a novel experience or being witness to a repetitious routine. Coyle (2009) uses the word *ignite* to define this aspect of initiating talent for development, while Willis (2010), coming from a neurological perspective, prefers to describe this inspiration phase as "curiosity sparked by a novelty," as the uniqueness in the situation literally causes the neurons to fire with electrochemical interactions that result in the cognitive search process. Both of these interpretations lend themselves to the idea that inspiration is like an explosion, when something snaps with a Boom! effect. Yet inspiration may also grow slowly, similar to planting a seed and nurturing it until it takes root. Shenk (2011) offers another perspective to this discussion that may simulate the seed of inspiration with his thesis that there is genius in all of us. Inspiration seems connected to these particular catalysts: aspirations, hallmarks, competiveness, and novelty.

In turn, evident in study after study (Colvin, 2008; Coyle, 2009; Ericsson & Pool, 2016b; Gladwell, 2008; Lemov et al., 2012; Rose, 2015; Shenk, 2011) is the necessity to provide the stature and steadfastness required of elite performers.

One student became so engrossed in physical science, fascinated by the concept of black holes, she told her 8th-grade teacher she wanted to become a world-famous physicist and discover more about the interplanetary origins. Her invigoration with this phenomenon is definitely quite ambitious for one so young. In fact, she exhibits a future vision of herself, stoking the fire each time she voices her aspirations to others.

Yet, in their journey to extraordinariness and elite performances, these individuals with maturing talents require constant, continual, and caring attention to invigorate their efforts with practice, coaching, and regular gradations of "reachfulness" (Coyle, 2009). This is what pushes their talent and propels them through hardships, failures, and disappointments, always looking and moving forward incrementally onward.

Instilled with the talent, over time, this desire, this dream, this aspiration, this nudging to "be the best" becomes part and parcel of the person's raison d'être. It cements the motivation that becomes deeply instilled in the person's psyche. These individuals are willing to do whatever it takes, to do things that others do not. Somehow, they have an element of invigoration that continues to sustain them. It's almost like they *have* to do it. Cautious of the possibility of burnout, Lemov et al. (2012) advocate an 80/20 rule in *Practice Perfect*, in which they practice key, coached elements 20% really well, instead of trying to do the "whole enchilada" each practice session.

These opening three chapters are intended to illuminate the critical element of motivation and the role it plays in developing expertise in any field. Ongoing motivational ploys boost the learners to keep them going full speed ahead until they consciously internalize the will, the drive, and the know-how to continually stay in the moment and keep themselves freshly inspired. And, most urgently, to acquire the precious resilience to persevere and do whatever it takes, whenever it is consciously needed, is the secret to a motivational influence. In closing, the motivational tactics of inspiring, invigorating, and instilling the drive to excel appear and grow in highly personal pathways, yet they are very much necessary ingredients for elite performances. With that in mind, there are extensive ideas about how teachers might formally and informally enhance student performance with truly inspired lessons, invigorating assignments and assessments, and methods to instill a passion and vigor for talent to grow and flourish.

CHAPTER 1

Inspire

A good teacher can inspire hope, ignite the imagination, and instill a love of learning.

—Brad Henry

Inspiration is as elusive as the illusions of a magician. Yet it is that powerful driver of hope, aspirations, and actions toward a goal. When uninspired, one may find work tedious and tiring; when inspired, one works with joyfulness and flow (Csikszentmihalyi, 2008). Just as stories of inspiration stir the heart and play with the mind, they do, indeed, bring action to bear on the dreams that are there. This action begins with stepping-stones and can lead the way toward spectacular achievements.

A short YouTube video of Misty Copeland reveals her journey to the pinnacle of the ballet world. While the context of the video is actually a promotion for Under Armour, her story nevertheless sheds light on the complexity of inspiration. In this case, instead of glowing commentary that inspires, Copeland weathered an avalanche of critiques about her deficit areas that would keep her from attaining her goal as a ballerina. However, all of the challenges delineated by the judges had a surprising, reverse effect on Misty as she somehow accepted the negative remarks as challenges to overcome. She persevered with those who supported her dreams, and against all odds, rose to the top of the field as prima ballerina of the American Ballet Theater. Her "I Will What I Want" video (Under Armour, 2014) hints at the self-confidence and belief in herself that has propelled Misty into the limelight.

In brief, the story of Misty Copeland illuminates how a "defining moment" can dramatically impact one's life journey. After an audition with a local ballet company at the age of 13, Misty received a heartbreaking rejection letter that spelled out in cruel detail her shortcomings as a budding ballerina:

> "unfortunately you have not been accepted into the ballet. . . . You have the wrong feet, your Achilles tendon is elongated, your torso is too long, you are too curvy, your bust is too big and you do not have the lines that reflect the classic body of a ballerina. Also, you are too old at thirteen to begin a career in ballet." (Under Armour, 2014)

In the YouTube clip, Misty dances, an indication of her triumph over a defining moment, evidence that she had achieved her early aspirations of greatness with the effusive energy and the graceful elegance of a star. She was a determined talent untapped; she was on the brink of greatness and she knew it, and she found the inspiration deep within herself and in a literal army of others along the way. Thus, her early disappointment did not discourage her as it might have with others.

DEFINING MOMENTS

"Defining moments" in life, are momentous occasions that leave an indelible mark on the heart and soul. They are those rare moments that inspire or cause one to rise to the challenge and recognize those special moments as a vision of possible future self. More often than not, these instances occur when someone else recognizes a young person's interest or developing ability and comments on it. Once the words are spoken, they are "in the air" and they take on a level of import not present before. In other situations, the learner has a moment that creates that first inner thought of self-potential: "I wonder if I can do that?" or "I want

"Defining moments" in life, are momentous occasions that leave an indelible mark on the heart and soul.

to do that" or "If they can do that, I can, too" or "I'm good at that, too," or "I want to do what they do." And the dream begins to take shape. In fact, it may be a watershed moment when one discovers a truth that could be life changing. One such moment entails self-awareness of a particular developing ability that is called out explicitly: "You have an amazing voice." It may be surprising how often an individual has not been recognized overtly with a comment on his or her talent or natural gift. In fact, a young person may even think that everyone has that same ability and not even realize that there is something very special that he or she possesses until it's actually called out and identified by others.

Lighting the Fire Within

On the other side of the coin, just as with Misty Copeland's story, a defining moment can be sparked by a comment that overtly challenges one's abilities. One young man's story of a life-changing moment involved a high school teacher who advised him that he was not "college material." In his retelling of this demoralizing moment, he talks about how it had instantly crushed his dream of becoming a PE instructor and high school coach. Yet it had somehow challenged him. Over many years, he worked to overcome that negative appraisal of his potential. He said that deep inside himself, he did not believe it was a true measure of what he could do, and in spite of that damaging opinion, he became determined to prove the comments false. As it happened, he did find support and champions along the way, who reinforced his belief in his abilities. This is a story of hard work, but it is also a story of a "growth mindset" as described by Dweck (2016) of someone who believes he can improve at anything.

"I Can" Mindset

Both of the above instances confirm stories related in the book *Mindset,* (Dweck, 2016) with many examples of defining moments, some negative, cementing the "fixed mindset." For example, a teacher's comment to a student like "You'll never be a good writer," despite our ballerina example, can undermine a student's confidence forever. Other examples from Dweck are quite positive, fostering what she calls a "growth mindset," with statements like: "You have shown that remarkable persistence you have as you tackled this challenge today" or "Your knack for finding a title is quite extraordinary." These two mindsets, fixed and growth, determine one's perspective on life and the life situations one encounters. The first mindset, a fixed mindset, was championed for years by the belief in the nature over nurture theory of development, which held that one is born with a certain amount of intelligence and/or talent that is unchangeable: You're either smart or you're not, and that's the way it is. Contrary to that theory is the nurture theory, advocating that one's natural abilities are enhanced by a nurturing environment or, in fact, may be diminished by the lack of one. It is in a nurturing environment that a growth mindset can flourish.

SOURCES OF INSPIRATION

To inspire one's self or to be inspired by another is where it all begins. Self-inspiration comes about quite incidentally at times, but in other cases there is a direct line to the spark that starts the burn. One student became so engrossed in physical science, fascinated by the concept of black holes, that she told her 8th-grade teacher she wanted to become a world famous physicist and discover more about the interplanetary origins. Her invigoration with this phenomenon is definitely quite ambitious for one so young. In fact, she exhibits a future vision of herself, stoking the fire each time she voices her aspirations to others.

> Self-inspiration comes about quite incidentally at times, but in other cases there is a direct line to the spark that starts the burn.

In another instance, William, a student in rural South Carolina, viewed a video of a volcano erupting and played the scene over and over again. When the teacher asked him what he was doing, he said, "I'm trying to figure it out. I want know how it came up from inside the earth." William smiled when she said, "You are always so curious. You should be a scientist. Geologists study the earth, you know." This kind of simple statement may be the nudge that makes the difference in a student's path.

Self-Inspired

Ralph W. Sockman's statement, "The larger the island of knowledge, the longer the shoreline of wonder," serves as a backdrop for this idea of self-inspired talent or talent recognized and inspired by another. As many agree, the more vast one's experiences, and the more varied one's background, the greater the opportunity for a seed of curiosity to surface and drive youngsters to pursue a particular interest. Intrigued, or even more, once involved, one often feels the need to explore the possibilities of this newly found interest or gift. This is why teachers try to expose their students to a variety of possible interests, skills, and potential passions. They become brokers of opportunities across many areas, offering students choices to pursue projects and independent studies. Teachers know to direct students toward many new zones of exploration, certainly to spark interests, but it may also uncover a lifelong interest for a student. To facilitate such discovery as the curriculum unfolds, "choice within a structure" is a guideline teachers often follow. As students work on South American culture, they can be allowed to choose one of the six areas of study: foods, music, sports, art, literature, or government. Simply by incorporating choice, exposure to multiple cultural arenas is possible.

Inspired by Experts

A 3rd-grader was glued to the screen when the high-diving competition was featured during the summer Olympics and turned to her parents to announce that she wanted to do that when she grew up. In fact, she enrolled in swimming and diving classes, and at the tender age of 10 is winning diving feats in her division. She is on her way, inspired merely from the images that evoked that elusive inner voice that somehow stays the course for her: "I want to do this. I can do this. I will do this. I am doing what I dreamed of doing."

A family member, parents, siblings, or close friends, or even a neighbor who knows the learner well, are often the ones who see the potential in a student that seems to stand out. When students or parents have shared this information, teachers can often find ways to reference and support students and show them potential applications within their learning to the passion that they are pursuing.

Inspired by Teachers, Coaches, and Mentors

By making the effort to know their students well as individuals, teachers' antennae can also pick up on students' talents and interests. They also recognize that they can mentor a gift that seems uniquely promising. When teachers see that spark of talent and comment on the potential, it can have a lasting impact on the student. If athletic coaches or performing arts instructors notice a particular skillfulness or spot a star-in-waiting, more often than not they act on that hunch. They may make a positive comment, or provide coaching feedback and even a correcting commentary that moves the player toward excellence. In any case, the interest is obvious and subsequent steps may be taken to ensure that the talent is recognized and nurtured.

Teachers often provide that catalyst for inspiring moments to occur. A young boy had been fascinated with dinosaurs from the time he got his first set of plastic dinosaur figurines. He was entranced with these prehistoric creatures, playing out action scenes with all kinds of imaginary predators. After seeing "Sue," the dinosaur replica that stands tall in the Field Museum in Chicago, on a 4th-grade field trip, he was unrelenting in his pursuit to learn everything he could about dinosaurs. This is an example of the power and authenticity of field trips, excursions, real-life interviews, and even bringing guest speakers into the classroom, which teachers plan and do throughout their lessons, that may touch a student in an inspiring way.

Through continued pursuits with digital media, film, online research, and summer camp at authentic archeological sites, that boy is now a keen and knowledgeable expert on dinosaurs. This summer as a college freshman he will work as an apprentice from Lewis and Clark College on his first authentic overseas archeological site in Italy. The seeds that are sometimes planted early on often sustain themselves in full-blown life passions and eventual careers.

Inspired by Peers

Even peers are known to inspire their classmates with a pat on the back or a high five, or some other kind of signal when they recognize an extraordinary talent or skill or just a sense of poise and confidence, whether it is in athletics, or writing, or drawing building designs for three-dimensional printing. Regardless of who sees the potential, their gestures and words champion talent and inspire the greatness that is obvious to these youngsters, and sometimes reveal to teachers abilities that they too can encourage.

VOICES

Supporting these stories of inspiring interests and possible passions are studies and cutting edge research, including overlapping and conflicting data that support or bump into others' views. Here we discuss specific influences from various authorities on inspiring, motivating, and igniting the passion needed to excel.

Csikszentmihalyi

Csikszentmihalyi (2008) wrote one of the seminal pieces of research on motivation and its component parts of inspiration and investment, originating the idea that when one enters a state of flow, the work is enhanced by powerful intrinsic motivation, extreme concentration, and an awareness of a sense of joyfulness. Time passes unnoticed as this total immersion consumes the learner. This relates to the concept of inspiration that is almost entirely within one's self, yet the passion comes with skillfulness and an increasing satisfaction with the work. It simulates that feeling of being "in the zone" when everything is syncing and the fluidity is real.

While not easily accessed in the classroom, the teacher can structure the time differently to foster genuine student engagement. Some schools, seeking to tap into the talents and needs of their students, suggest this simple, yet innovative model, called "The Genius Hour." It is a stunning example of intentional and purposeful time allotment for students to pursue high-interest projects with vim and vigor. Started in the workplace with the high-tech companies including Google, Apple, and Yahoo, the idea is to inspire creativity and innovative excellence in products and performances.

Ericsson, Krampe, and Tesch-Römer

Ericsson, Krampe, and Tesch-Römer (1993) developed ideas in their early work about the nature or nurture of talent, and their findings weighed heavily in favor of nurture through deliberate, measured, intentional practice routines, installed across thousands of hours. The oversimplified term attached to Ericsson et al., but coined by Gladwell (2008), was the rule of 10,000 hours to become an expert. In this work, there are also references to motivating factors including intense concentration, a deliberate focus, and a sense of self that is ignited as the process unfolds and makes deep and lasting dedication possible.

Gladwell

Yet this iteration of deliberate practice had a huge impact on public awareness and is widely quoted throughout coaching sessions in sports, music, the arts, and even in acquiring academic acumen. Again, as in the case of Ericsson and others, while Gladwell's (2008) presentation of facts may seem more appropriate in the discussion of practice in Part II, it is also inextricably linked to inspired motivation. This helps one understand how coaches, mentors, and teachers serve to drive students to persevere, with grit and with joy. As the genius Thomas Alva Edison (n.d.) remarked, "Success is 10% inspiration, 90% perspiration!" Both count. Without the inspiration, the perspiration may never have a chance to develop. Yet, if it's only perspiration, lacking any lasting inspiration, it may be short-lived. It follows that motivation and inspired action seem likely companions to the pure grit and nose-to-the-grindstone mentality. In fact, throughout the chapters, readers will notice that the elements of practice, inspiration, and masterful coaching often overlap in the discussion of each element.

Ericsson and Pool

In a recent publication Ericsson and Pool (2016a) updated their work on hours and practice when they critiqued an excerpt in a journal headline. In this document they offer a substantive rebuttal to Gladwell: "Malcolm Gladwell Got Us Wrong: Our Research Was Key to the 10,000-Hour Rule, But Here's What Got Oversimplified." Ericsson and Pool (2016b) then go on to elaborate factors that are necessary to make those 10,000 hours a true road to talent development in a comprehensive treatment in which they coin the term *peak*:

> Peak discusses how dedicated training with deliberate practice is why it works as well as it does, and how experts apply it to produce their extraordinary abilities. According to these experts, the reason some people are amazingly good at what they do is because they work harder . . . a lot harder. In examining the issue of innate endowment and what role it might play in limiting how far some people can go in attaining expert performance . . . [and] while the principles of deliberate practice were discovered by studying expert performers, the principles themselves can be used by anyone who wants to improve at anything, even if just a little bit (pp. xxii–xxiii).

The development of expertise to extraordinary levels of elite performances is coming into its own as a viable methodology. Ericsson and Pool open the door for school and personal applications when they say, "the principles themselves can be used by anyone who wants to improve at anything, even if just a little."

With that schema in mind, findings on the power of purposeful practice are delineated in detail in Part II of this book, "Practicing: Engineer to Develop Expertise," illustrating the inextricable linkages between the study of peak performance and the study of instructional best practices in motivating and sustaining excellence through ongoing, incremental practice and motivational and coaching/feedback cycles.

Dweck

Dweck's discussion in *Mindset: The New Psychology of Success* (2006), noted earlier, contributes to the conversation on talent and expertise, with her perspective on explicit strategies to inspire growth mindsets in our youngsters in and out of the classroom. With the belief that growth mindsets are at least partially responsible for building and instilling confidence, this is important work that many schools and educators know. With the known element of plasticity of the human brain, the fact that brains change as they learn, it becomes more apparent than ever that our academic communities need to foster this motivating growth mindset in youngsters to propel their belief in themselves as "learning able." Youngsters can embrace the inspiring notion that human beings can learn, practice, and strive to achieve the level of accomplishments they desire. Greatness is possible with an "I Can" attitude.

> Greatness is possible with an "I Can" attitude.

Coyle

Coyle (2009) connects to this work also, as he describes how it is possible to build an ecosystem for developing the science of expertise. Deliberate, coached practices, with many iterations, precise coaching feedback at the micro level, and frequent doses of motivational tactics create that miniature ecosystem that helps to build the myelin that underscores the automaticity and developing excellence of the skills. As we explained in the introduction, the myelin on each brain cell wraps itself around the axon and in doing so strengthens and speeds up the performance each and every time it is revisited. Understanding these and other elements of developing expertise affords teachers the great satisfaction of laying precious foundations for student expertise to bud, blossom, and flower.

Duckworth

In this vein of study A. Duckworth (2016) asks, What makes super-high achievers? According to her writings, it's not just the stick-to-itiveness, or the grit and resilience she writes about, but combinations of stamina, a sense of purpose, and a deepening commitment to an area of achievement. This sentiment is echoed by educators, who know that the level of excellence and expertise is a synchronization of multiple components, rationed in individuals in varied proportions.

> "Sometimes, the more talented you are, the less gritty you are." (Angela Duckworth, 2017, pp. 2–7)

Rose

Complementing Coyle's discussion in *The Talent Code*, Todd Rose's (2015) *The End of Average: How We Succeed in a World That Values Sameness* reports interesting data about what we know as average, and contrasts two words commonly heard in classrooms and staff rooms: *average* and *excellent*.

Rose contends that using the value of average as our standard yardstick for measurement—from one's height, weight, and size to one's IQ, skillfulness and acumen in sports, size of our families, home prices, and even the amount of our grocery bills—is not really that accurate or that helpful.

A story told by Rose (2015) illustrates dire fallacies about the value of using average as our ground zero. In the 1940s the U.S. Air Force decided to use average measurements of hundreds of pilots to determine the specs for designing and building airplane cockpits. And they did. But, after a series of plane accidents in the first year, when the actual data of the pilot participants was compared to the actual sizing of the cockpit specifications, not a single pilot met the criteria that had been used to determine the "average." Not one of the pilots was average! It was necessary to go back to the drawing board and recalibrate everything with adjustable features, particularly the pilots' seats. Rose questions, with action-laden data, if this concept of average serves to motivate or diminish student performance. In truth, it seems barely possible within the frame of this premise that averaging skillfulness would not impact motivation. Kamenetz (2016) also comments on the idea of average:

> We have a brutally standardized system. It doesn't matter what your interests are, what job you want, everyone takes the same courses in roughly the same time and at the end of the course you get ranked. . . . The idea that someone is going to click a stopwatch, compare you to other kids in your class, and the kids with the best grades can get the best jobs, that's not a good deal. I want my two boys to figure out what they love and what they're good at and be exposed to things and be able to turn that into a job. (Kamenetz, 2016)

Shenk

Confirming other viewpoints, Shenk (2011) draws from several scientific fields to provide a compelling look at human potential in *The Genius in All of Us: New Insights into Genetics, Talent, and IQ*. Shenk points out that "our genes are not a blueprint that dictates individual destinies" (p. 49). Rather, our potential is influenced by the combination of our genes and outside stimuli. This is another reaffirmation that the biology of the human being and the life experiences one encounters are heralded as the combination that unlocks the gifts that have been given. Of course, that genius in us all may need uncovering, understanding, and unusual mentoring to expose that potential that is there.

How to (Ruin) or Inspire a Kid . . . it begins with a simple faith that each child has enormous potential and that it is up to us to muster whatever resources we can to exploit that potential. Rather than wonder if [the) child is among the "gifted" chosen few . . . believe deeply in the extraordinary potential. (p.128)

Willis

The work of Judy Willis (2006), neuroscientist and teacher, includes a broad and beautiful methodology from the science on how the brain learns. In work that bridges neuroscience and teaching, her discussion of the science of motivating and inspiring learners is strikingly on target. It harkens back to what educators already know about the temporary impact of extrinsic motivation. In this case, extrinsic motivation used cleverly is a mere catalyst to spark a natural intrinsic motivator called "curiosity." Willis's ideas about classroom instruction align with brain-friendly behaviors on the part of the teacher and show that students benefit from the natural instincts of their brains as "meaning-making machines."

Willis's work suggests that once the teacher acts in a motivating or inspiring way, with a novel opening or compelling hook to her lesson, students' curiosity is aroused. Once they are teased with an unknown, a telling prop, an intriguing challenge, or humorous role play, youngsters want to know more. They want to discover, discuss, and subsequently describe and define what it is they can learn about their world.

Inspiration, how we motivate kids, how we hook them, how we invite them gingerly into the learning in brain-friendly ways, is at the heart of Willis's work. Willis's findings, drawn from her remarkable career as a neuroscientist turned middle school science teacher, gives her this dichotomy of perspectives. She opens doors to know what occurs inside the brain and how that signals actions outside the brain that spark the learner's need to know. Here is a bit of her thinking that has led her to this theory of tapping into the natural science systems of the brain:

Although the brain is an amazing organ, it's not equipped to process the billions of bits of information that bombard it every second. Filters in your brain protect it from becoming overloaded. These filters control the information flow so that only approximately 2,000 bits of information per second enter the brain. (Willis, 2009, p. 1)

Figure 1.1. Inspiring Students

Step 1. Arouse Curiosity
Step 2. Foster Investigations
Step 3. Guide Validation

Source: Willis (2006).

Further explanation illuminates the importance of this information. The sensory information enters the brain and chooses one of two routes. It either goes directly to the prefrontal cortex, the "thinking brain," to process and reflect. Or the incoming data goes to the "automatic brain" that reacts instinctively. This reactive brain may cause the brain to ignore information, fight against it, or avoid it. In these cases, it is unlikely that the brain will process the incoming input in any cognitive way.

Willis (2009) describes three filters that control what your brain takes in: (1) the reticular activation system (RAS), the first filter, a mechanism that perceives something different in the environment; (2) the limbic system with the amygdala, that is like a train-routing station for emotions; and (3) the chemical neurotransmitter, dopamine, which sends electrical messages across the synapses between brain cells. In the case of the dopamine, it is a feel-good message that increases the likelihood of openness to learning.

Most important to this conversation on inspiration is knowing that the RAS acts as the gatekeeper of the primitive brain, a reflexive mechanism that immediately alerts the brain that something is different, that there is some novelty (a "danger on the horizon" kind of novelty in Darwin's theory of survival of the fittest), and this sensory signal causes an arousal state.

The RAS signal creates an alert, a desire to know more, a curiosity of what might occur. This is what Willis discusses in determining what works best on the outside of the brain, in terms of getting student attention, getting a focused alertness, if you will, as an effective teaching technique. She understands how teachers can create a sense of novelty to trigger the brain to go into search action. Good teachers do this when they think about creative ways to get students' attention at the beginning of a lesson.

In her career-long study, Willis applies her findings from the lab about how the brain works best to her instructional work in a 7th-grade science classroom. As shown in Figure 1.1, her findings indicate that by using this novelty, a natural curiosity is inherently sparked for students. Once this occurs, they want to know more, and students will actually initiate their own investigations until they hit a desired validation point.

One way to arouse curiosity in a classroom is the use of props. For example, when the teacher enters the classroom dressed in the recognizable white coat of a medical lab technician, it inspires curiosity and inquiry. She is simply changing something dramatically, so when students enter the classroom they notice. In fact, they are buzzing about it. "What's this? Why are you dressed like a doctor? What are we going to do?" Her response, now that she has hooked them and has their undivided attention, is, "Talk about what you think I have in mind," unleashing a flood of ideas that flow across the room. While she uses this to promote questions and inquiries, at the same time she is inspiring students as they realize their natural capacity to generate fresh new ideas of their own, such as a study of the human body or human cells, or even biographies of scientists, or a genetic code unit, or maybe even a field trip to a hospital or lab. Their inventive ideas are intriguing to them and they are eager to know exactly what the lab coat reference is all about. In fact, they can't wait to find out. They are hooked, attentive, and wanting to know. This is the first step: curiosity. The second is a micro-investigation, and then a tiny link to validation. This focuses on the inspiring part. There are two other big pieces not stressed here: investigating and validating. That is where the actual teaching occurs.

This simple sequence of brain activity is the curiosity and motivation teachers strive to generate in their students every day. At best this phenomenon of the brain arousal, the inherent curiosity to know, describes an actual "Aha! moment." Willis's findings affirm the power of student-centered models of inquiry learning that seem to linger in the wings of the more traditional classroom. These forms of learning have the capacity to boost learning, develop student confidence in developing expertise, and show them new areas of intellectual pursuit.

IMPACT

How inspiration impacts the development of expertise for anyone who wants to improve or excel at a skill, a talent, or a passionate interest is, of course, one of the three most important messages of this text. Knowing how to spark the motivation to learn, to initiate a natural starter for kids, can be a significant turning point for teachers and their students.

> Knowing how to spark the motivation to learn, to initiate a natural starter for kids, can be a significant turning point for teachers and their students.

This may be especially true for those who are ready to move from the traditional, teacher-directed classrooms to student-centered classrooms in which students, motivated by inquiring minds, are eager to dig into the learning. In fact, that is the purpose of this chapter, to share with readers how to initiate student-centered inquiry models and use student choice to invite ownership of the learning experience and develop academic, social, and personal expertise to the greatest extent possible.

With this in mind, the teacher learns how to champion student agency by shifting responsibilities, and even the direction of a study investigation, over to the student teams. Willis has tried-and-true tips and full-blown strategies that target student involvement and authentic engagement from the students as they proceed through the biologically induced steps of the human brain that naturally seek knowledge and understanding.

To reiterate: In Step 1, the teacher arouses student curiosity by initiating a novelty or surprising prompt that students cannot help but notice. In Step 2, student teams are encouraged to investigate, explore, and experiment to satisfy their curiosity. Finally, in Step 3, the students are guided into a validation process that shows evidence of their findings and their conclusion to the experience.

Much like a "talent whisperer," the teacher's role becomes more facilitator of student learning than teacher of student knowledge. Yet, clearly, the teaching of skills and concepts when needed, particularly with minilessons, is part of this process as students learn how to take over more of the responsibility for their own learning. In fact, the structured minilessons on content, research, online searches, outlining, note-taking, organizing information into displays, and even effective presentation skills become teachable moments that matter to the team progress. Learning takes on a rare relevance when kids are put in charge. Of course, this is as relevant for individual students or exceptionally talented youngsters as it is for classroom instruction/coaching strategy.

Willis actually shares a plethora of coaching remarks that are invaluable as teachers move to this more dynamic classroom model of "guide on the side." Scan the strategies seen in Figure 1.2 that Willis has discovered through her work. Revisit the ones you already use or implement the ones that make perfect sense to you or the ones you definitely want to try.

PROFESSIONAL LEARNING COMMUNITIES DISCUSSION QUESTIONS

- Who or what has inspired you as a teacher over the years?
- How do teachers help students find their talent or proclivity for something? Hypothesize.
- Share your take on the nature versus nurture argument about a performance talent. Justify.

Figure 1.2. RAS Gatekeeper

I. To Cause Arousal, Alertness, to Focus Attention

- Say student's name before asking a question
- Incorporate real-world connections
- Maximize personal relevance with meaningful reference
- Gather and use background knowledge about students
- Connect class work and homework
- Challenge the brain to arouse it

II. Limbic System/Hippocampus

- Use emotions for memory to enhance learning
- Use humor to stimulate emotions for deeper learning
- Review and practice to reboot and create positive feelings
- Reteach using motions or actions to ground information
- Use pairs, partner work, dialogues to stimulate emotions
- Provide choice and options to connect with emotions

III. Dopamine

- Foster the optimal state for learning, remembering, applying
- Focus on positive interactions and feedback on effort
- Pursue closure to task for sense of accomplishment
- Structure physical activities for movement that energizes
- Have students appreciate partner with statement: I appreciate . . .
- Reflect on best part of project to foster good feelings

Source: Willis (2009).

PROFESSIONAL LEARNING EXERCISE: "INSPIRE-SPEAK"

"It'll Never Fly, Wilbur!"

Dweck (2007) talks about motivational moments, when one is truly flattered by a verbal compliment or implicit positive feedback in the form of a pat on the back, an outstretched hand, or a high five or even an actual handwritten note of appreciation for an earnest effort. The acknowledgment, no matter how subtle or how overt, never goes unnoticed by the learner. These are the moments that can turn lives around. They are the tiny moments that say we are not only okay, we are special. And it feels good. It spurs kids on to do even better next time. And it doesn't take much to do this in genuine and authentic interactions with students.

Yet sometimes the world appears to be a little more aloof, or removed, or even too cynical for those simple gestures of kindness and encouragement. Think about the frequency of put-downs by family, peers, and colleagues when someone excitedly shares a thought about something they want to do. Do these put-downs ring a bell? "It'll never fly, Wilbur." "Not a bright idea, Thomas." "It's not relative, Albert." It's just so easy to brush them off with "Been there, done that" kinds of dismissive remarks. Just for the exercise, working with a partner, have students generate a put-down about a famous person of accomplishment, similar to these. Tell them to produce at genius level.

That's a Good Idea!

Now that that is over and everyone has enjoyed the creative moment, what if we turned that negative into a positive, and instituted a "That's a Good Idea" rule? Think about the difference in tenor and mood and actual motivation to act when someone says, "That's a good idea because . . ." and gives a sound, viable reason for genuine consideration of the idea. To spark "Inspire-Speak" in the classroom, within the family circle, and around the friends' hangout, use the "That's a Good Idea" rule and see what happens.

Even though it may start out as kind of cynical and sarcastic, "Thhhh-at's a Good Idea," the positive words keep coming. There is some recognition even in these early rounds, that it is not as easy to compliment an idea as it is to put it down with one smart-aleck swipe. But, also, the smiles, the upward fluctuations in energy and enthusiasm, the flurry of activity that seem to flourish when the words are inspiring rather than demeaning are also obvious. It feels good.

School leaders and classroom teachers, both real and fictional, are forever inspiring others. In films or in real life, they exemplify traits of creative, persistent, risk takers with spirit and vision. These educators show how they inspire others to be all they are capable of being. They are the ones who see something special in others and have the wherewithal, the caring and kindness, and the dedication and commitment to remark on what they recognize as unusual or beyond the ordinary skillfulness and talent. They see the potential for all youngsters as learners, on the brink of greatness. One never knows when students have moments of breakthrough. Thus, effective teachers are never remiss in recognizing and inspiring students to succeed.

CHAPTER 2

Invigorate

Don't you find that work, if you love it, is actually really invigorating?

—Cate Blanchett

Invigorate literally means "to give vigor to; fill with life and energy; rejuvenate." It derives from the concept "to expand" and that is exactly what appears to happen. All of us have experienced that kind of second wind. It is that lift and momentum to keep going with an invigorated feeling of empowerment. After feeling exhausted and drained, one suddenly is enlivened and exhibits an enormous surge of energy. Something may trigger the rejuvenation, like a change in location or a change in activity, or it may just erupt in response to the earlier excitement. Whatever it is, it seems to follow an ironic truth: The more one does, the more one can do.

An example of this kind of invigoration is found in the elite athlete Michael Jordon. Back in the day, Jordan was reported to be tireless and was known for needing fewer than 4 hours of sleep a night. He was a gifted athlete, but his drive and will to compete enabled him to become one of the most dominant sportsmen in history.

It is rumored that Michael Jordan practiced more than anyone else, was always up for another scrimmage, or a card game, a round of golf, shooting baskets far into the night while his teammates were done and gone. Ericsson and Pool (2016a) reference this continued energy as maintenance, yet in light of Jordon's remarkable level of energy throughout the night following a rigorous and demanding game, it was far beyond maintenance. It was self-invigorating and self-renewing. In Jordon's case, it was an extreme state of self-motivation. It was a self-fulfilling prophecy that flowed like a humming mantra: "The more one does, the more one can do."

To put this into terms for invigorating the students in our classrooms, it is easy to rally students with a similar trigger. By planning a show or exhibition of their work or a demonstration of their performances, students are motivated with renewed energy as they prepare to showcase their work. The invitation to show their artwork, or perform in the PE demonstration, or participate in the school musical performance, or the school poetry fest, or even preparation for parent conferences seems to do the trick. Humans are motivated to act by enticements that matter to them: endeavors that are relevant and raise the bar on the mundane routines of the everyday class work. Whatever teachers can do to create that kind of inspired, invigorating action keeps kids at the top of their game.

One example that illustrates this common invigoration of spirit and energy is the announcement in a charcoal drawing class that the art students were invited to show some of their work at an upcoming art show in a gallery. The idea of a public showing certainly brought out the "spit and polish" as the entire class was enlivened, even for those who would choose not to show. Collecting, selecting, reflecting, framing, and naming were all invigorating endeavors that would put a renewed spirit on the work and on the showcase pieces.

CHALLENGE TO PERSIST AND TO PEAK

Perhaps one of the greatest challenges is to find the will, the courage, and the undefeatable attitude to persist. To challenge oneself to exceed the comfort zone and to push beyond one's self-perceived outer limits is to practice with untethered faith and fidelity. Reaching beyond anything done previously, always knocking on that door of a new record, a farther reach than ever reached before—what Coyle (2009) called "reachfulness"—is what "peaking" involves. *Reachfulness* is the constant pounding in one's head to stretch and stretch and stretch to that new limit, no matter how miniscule. It is a new high. The role of the teacher, coach, or mentor is to keep tipping the learner forward from passivity toward reachable action. It is a continuous cycle that maintains and sustains skillfulness, yet also scores a plus within the learner for the new mark that has been reached. This requires constant dissatisfaction with the current specs or data and a yearning to do one's personal best, each and every outing. It is exhausting on the one hand, and on the other it is exhilarating and truly invigorated by the tiny, barely noticeable successes that keep the learner moving ever forward.

Digging deeper into this concept of "invigoration," one uncovers some interesting findings that are both true to experience and supported by clinical research. In fact, invigorating inspired talent takes on many forms. In particular, the following four categories seem to invigorate and energize: aspirations, competitiveness, novelty, and hallmarks.

ASPIRATIONS, COMPETITIVENESS, NOVELTY, AND HALLMARKS

Learners are invigorated by their own aspirations for greatness, their innate competitiveness to exceed, the forever occurring novelty that appears constantly as they grow in expertise and also as they become aware of changes and advancements in their field and, finally, by the highly notable hallmarks that punctuate the successes of their endeavors. A deeper look at each of these illuminates the power and force of invigorating elements in the making of champions and in the satisfaction of students as they see and value themselves as learners and pursuers of their interests.

Aspirations to Be "Somebody"

Aspirations are often sparked and sustained by proximity to role models, studies of figures of historical significance, and from the performers' own self-directed and self-cultivated inner spirit that constructively drives that person to excel. It has to be there for the performer or learner to succeed to these highest of heights. It comes from way down deep inside them, and it is the personal vision that propels them to strive each and every day.

Examples of aspiring stars are plentiful in various sports and in the performing arts. Students gravitate to these models naturally. As a young golfer, Tiger Woods kept a list on his wall of some of the accomplishments of the greatest golfer of the time, Jack Nicklaus, and used this as the list that he wanted to beat: "the first time [Jack] broke 40, the first time he broke 80, the first golf tournament he ever won, first time he ever won the state amateur, first time he won the U.S. Amateur, and the first time he won the U.S.

Open. . . . It was all age-related" (Woods, quoted in Chase, 2015). Beating the accomplishments of the best in his field was his goal. This is the kind of adulation and serious commitment that comes from role models.

Just as prevalent are students in typical school situations. There are youngsters who yearn to be the top of their class in academic standings, or those who aspire to have significant leadership roles as class president or editor of the school newspaper or creator of the class blog. There are those who audition earnestly for the lead in the school musical, or volley for notoriety as scorekeeper on the junior varsity basketball team. Aspiration to excel, to live up to the standards of someone recognized and honored with a particular stature are part of students growing up and following their own special interests that eventually lead them to their chosen pathway.

Competiveness and Accomplishments

Competiveness is for many a prerequisite for developing excellence and true expertise. Fueled by incremental accomplishments, wins, and celebrations, these are the momentary catalysts that drive the talented one. They intermittently accelerate the personal push and renewed energy that is needed to continue full speed ahead. To mix the metaphor, the contests become stepping-stones that allow the learners to get closer and closer, one step at a time on the way to their ultimate, envisioned goal at that stage of their journey.

There are still others for whom pure pursuit of a goal is sufficient, or who pursue a goal in a new field where there are few to no competitors. Interestingly, Coyle names "Tip #51 Keep Your Big Goals Secret" (2012, p. 112). One study showed that by announcing your goal, there seems to be a trigger in the mind that feels like it is already accomplished, and youngsters quit their project work much earlier than those who had not announced their end goal. However, highly competitive players in sports and politics often proclaim their projected "win" for the very opposite reason, to scare off opponents and set the stage for a big win. Prizefighter and heavyweight champion Muhammad Ali is considered to be the greatest heavyweight boxer of all time. He was known for his poetic proclamations about the impending wins: "Float like a butterfly, sting like a bee," "It will be a killer, and a chiller, and a thriller, when I get the gorilla in Manila," "I done wrestled with an alligator, I done tussled with a whale; handcuffed lightning, thrown thunder in jail; only last week, I murdered a rock, injured a stone, hospitalized a brick; I'm so mean I make medicine sick."

In more traditional examples in school situations, youngsters may feel confident enough to say, "I'm going to ace this exam. I know it because I studied a lot for this." Or they might be more demure as suggested by the study cited earlier, and competitive students, highly likely to make the top grade, may simply say nothing aloud and wait to see if they accomplish at the level they wanted. Sometimes, they are not comfortable with the bragging, or they are sensitive to the feelings of fellow students. Students who enjoy the competition may be more vocal simply because they often have the high self-esteem that accompanies success. However, regardless of the stance students take, those who have a knack for competing may become more vocal as they begin to taste the flavor of success more frequently. As the saying goes, "Success breeds success." And at the end of the day, competition breeds winners.

Novelty Renews Commitment

Novelty is another key element in developing expertise and plays a major role as the individual is excited and invigorated by novelty and newness or some unusual aspect of their passionate endeavors. It is conventional wisdom that the brain is designed to experience novelty through a naturally occurring alert system triggered by the amygdala, the "excitement center" in the brain. When the human brain notices something on the horizon, something that seems different, out of the ordinary, then survival of the fittest (Spencer, 1898, p. 444) kicks in, and the emotional system goes on high alert. It is innately reflexive in the most basic way in order to alert the human of danger or opportunity, and in the end preserve the species. With that excitement comes a flow of adrenalin and a spurt of real energy.

As noted earlier, in the real world today, this alert system is still activated by novelty and registered in the brain as something to be excited about. This is what happens with novelty and change for the student who is invigorated by the simplest of changes.

In school classrooms students rise to the occasion when they know they have clear and significant responsibility to succeed and carry the team or themselves to completion of the project, or a response to a challenge that matters for their class standing. Yes, even a relay team game can trigger invigorated efforts by all. Students want to do their part and they will give their very best effort because they are integral to the final outcome. Novel situations spark renewal and seem to create particular watershed moments that spark rejuvenation, commitment, and the kind of "whatever it takes" effort needed for that final hurrah.

Hallmarks Celebrated

Hallmarks are the fourth element that seems to invigorate efforts beyond the norm for already outstanding performers. These hallmarks are interviews, awards, promotions, celebrations, and notoriety. It seems that any attention is better than none to keep humans invigorated, motivated, and ready to go the distance. To be more specific about what is meant by hallmarks, think of the school's student awards ceremony every spring or the classroom practice of honoring a different student each week with an entire bulletin board featuring the student as a star and noting their interests and accomplishments, contributions to the classroom and larger community. One teacher brings a large bouquet to class on the last day of school and awards one flower to each student, publicly recognizing contributions and good characteristics of each in a closing award ceremony. Students want to excel and they are invigorated by positive recognition of any sort: certificates of attendance, achievement, or outstanding performances. These are simple motivators that are common in school settings. Imagine the energy generated when students are interviewed by the school paper or mentioned during the morning announcements over the intercom for some accomplishment. Think of the many opportunities available to motivate students to excel, to invigorate them with the kind of energy it takes to succeed and to excel.

Because we know that inspired students must be invigorated to maintain, sustain, and accelerate efforts, it behooves us as teachers to provide support and accountability for invigorating with exciting and spontaneous events that keep students raring to go. The goal is to make school and learning so compelling that students want to be there; they are concerned that they might miss something important or, better yet, something really intriguing.

VOICES

Several years of working hard on implementation of the college and career readiness standards consumed schools across the country, and many have seen the fruits of their labor. Principals were leading the challenge, teachers were making substantive changes with standards-based lessons, and students were responding with emergent, yet definite, signs of improvement in achievement. Even with all the small and continual successes, however, schools were not feeling the joyfulness of a grand school experience.

Coyle

Coyle's (2009) words offer a counterbalancing hope and excitement about what is possible in nurturing student talent with practice radically different from current practice regimes. The concepts of igniting learners' interests, teaching them the power of deliberate practice routines, and masterfully coaching them as they progress, every step of the way, are truly designed for breakthroughs in student ownership of their own personalized learning, pride in the efforts that drive them, and a nurturing a sense of self-esteem that sustains their success-driven future endeavors.

Coyle addresses the concept of "primal cues," the idea that "They've picked up something in their environment that's made them say, 'Yes, that's for me'" (Coyle, 2009, p. 103). At some point very early on, they had a crystalizing experience that brings the idea to the fore, that says, "'I am a musician.' That idea is like a snowball rolling downhill." (2009, p. 104). For hard evidence of this phenomenon, see Coyle's (2009) discussion, using the Watkin's Performance Scale. In brief, Watkin asked his music students, prior to beginning their lessons, "How long do you think you'll play your new instrument?" The scale ranges from short-term, to medium-term to long-term. Interestingly, those who made a long-term commitment outperformed all others, regardless of practice time. A seed had already been planted and a sprig was already sprouting.

Dweck

Dweck (2007) cites the involvement of parents, teachers, and coaches as extremely instrumental in shaping growth mindsets with their youngsters, with messages that signal, "You are a developing person and I am interested in your development" (p. 172). She cautions that students may hear praise differently from what is intended. "You learned that so quickly. You're so smart," may be heard by the student, in his interpretation, "If I don't learn something quickly, I'm not smart" (Dweck, 2007, pp. 174, 175). She recommends strongly that positive comments on effort and the growth and development concepts are more powerful for invigorating youngsters' motivation.

Ericsson and Pool

Peak, the most recent publication by Ericsson and Pool (2016b), frames the concept of the science of expertise as something that is quite attainable. In brief, these authors dispel two age-old ideas that have surrounded conventional thinking about talent. First, they tackle the belief that innate talent is necessary in order to excel, and they also emphasize that "There are no shortcuts . . . expert performers develop their extraordinary abilities through years and years of dedicated practice . . . [particularly] deliberate practice" (p. 207).

They identify a moment in the development of expertise and the determination to achieve it: "Generally, when they're in their early or mid-teens,

Figure 2.1. Three Types of Drive
___

Motivation 1.0 Drive: We were trying to survive

Motivation 2.0 Drive: Way to improve-reward good, punish bad

Motivation 3.0 Drive: Innate autonomy and Type I behavior

Motivation 1.0: an early form of motivation driven by the survival mode;

Motivation 2.0: commonly accepted form of extrinsic punishment & reward;

Motivation 3.0: an emergent form of motivation focuses on the universal power
   of intrinsic motivation that can be harnessed.
___

Source: Pink (2009).

future experts make a major commitment to becoming the best that they can
be" (Ericsson & Pool, 2016b, p. 192), and it can be assumed that it signals
remarkable internal invigoration for the goal.

Pink

On the subject of motivation, Pink's (2009) book *Drive: The Surprising
Truth About What Motivates Us*, offers in Chapter 1 "The Rise and Fall of
Motivation," a perspective on the critically misunderstood concepts of intrinsic and extrinsic motivation that speaks to how teachers can invigorate motivation over the long term. Pink's overriding premise is that carrots and sticks
more often than not don't work. Rather, there is great power in intrinsic
motivation. Yet it is so frequently overlooked because there is little real understanding of this elusive element of personal, internally driven motivation.
Pink suggests three types of drive (Figure 2.1) that include Motivation1.0
Drive, Motivation 2.0, Drive, and Motivation 3.0 Drive.

  Pink talks about why Motivation 3.0, Intrinsic Desires, works. He feels
that it works best and proceeds to develop that argument, as he describes
how Intrinsic Desires outperforms Motivation 2.0 Extrinsic Desires. While
Type I is both naturally and environmentally made, individuals influenced
by Type I do not distain money or recognition, and Type I, 1.0, promotes
physical and mental well-being. These qualities are not always present in motivation that is entirely driven by Type II, 2.0, Extrinsic Drive, that depends
on the system of punishments and rewards that often are not personalized to
the talents and needs of the individuals.

  Subsequently, the discussion in Pink's text leads to particular measures
teachers can take to foster Type III, 3.0, Intrinsic Drive, in their students'

motivation. These measures include making a list of "NO" items, or "your own agenda of avoidance." He says that the things you decide *not* to do are as important as the things you decide to do. He also provides a self-test on the state of FLOW, or how immersed students are in an endeavor by entering a state of FLOW (Csikszentmihalyi, 2008). In turn, strategies from Clare Boothe Luce and her brilliant advice to "only ask big questions," beautifully illustrate what she means about having the big picture and, at the same time, paying attention to details (see Pink, 2009, p. 154).

Rose

Rose (2015) offers another perspective. He shows statistically that absolutely no one is average. Instead he promotes the Jaggedness Principle to explain his theory.

> The first principle of individuality is the "Jaggedness Principle." This principle holds that we cannot use one-dimensional thinking to understand something that is complex and jagged. What precisely is Jaggedness? A quality is jagged if it meets two criteria. First, it must involve multiple dimensions. Second, these dimensions must be weakly related to one another. Jaggedness . . . is about almost every human characteristic that we care about—including talent, intelligence, character, creativity and so on . . . is jagged. (p. 82)

Rose (2015) uses the example of a simple question: Which man is bigger? But instead of a simple answer, think about the many dimensions of size: girth, height, weight, as well as other dimensions such as shoulders, waist, chest, reach, and so on. It is an amazing revelation that comparing one's size is as complex as that, yet it makes perfect sense if you actually look at the scientific data.

> Rose (2015) offers another perspective. He shows statistically that absolutely no one is average. Instead he promotes the Jaggedness Principle to explain his theory.

In essence, Rose adheres to the concept of Ericsson and Pool (2016b), Gladwell (2008), Coyle (2009), and others who believe that talent consists of variables that matter and are in unique combinations in each individual. In addition, Rose implicitly supports the idea that there is genius in all of us, just as Shenk (2011) suggests. His work speaks to developing expertise and honing for excellence in all student performances. In a summary comment about uniqueness versus sameness, he comments that "We all walk the road less traveled" (Rose, 2015, p. 123). Thus, we all have genius in us, if uniqueness versus sameness is how genius is delineated.

It may be a new perspective for some, but the following comments do help clarify what Rose means.

He reports an example from the work of Karen Adolph (cited in Rose, 2015), in which she notes that even in the most primary task, such as learning to walk, there is not actually a "normal pathway, but rather, this researcher found no less than twenty-five different pathways infants followed, each in his own unique movement patterns, all of them leading to walking. . . . Every baby solves the problem of movement in her own unique way" (Rose, 2015, p. 126).

Rose also prompts us to look at the "pace of excellence." Rather than continuing our thinking that faster is better (whiz kid, quick study, quick win), he suggests that every person learns in his or her own way and at his or her own pace. This is important and probably controversial thinking when we look at invigorating students to stay motivated and continue to progress toward excellence. As Rose (2015) notes, "The architecture of our education system is simply not designed to accommodate such individuality, and it therefore fails to nurture the potential and talent of all students" (p. 133).

Shenk

Shenk (2011) reinforces the mindset work of Dweck (2006) in his discussion of the human brain and especially of plasticity, giving some intriguing facts:

1. Human brains change through a process called plasticity.
2. Brains are built for challenge and adaptation.
3. Babies are designed to change their minds when faced with data (Meltzoff, cited in Shenk 2011).
4. There is evidence that peers have more influence on character than even parents do (Harris, cited in Shenk, 2011).
5. Fostering patience and persistence, as well as embracing failure, has invigorating effects on sustaining and maintaining motivation.
6. All experiences lead to peak performances and excellence in student endeavors.

Colvin

Colvin (2008), in *Talent Is Overrated: What Really Separates World-Class Performers from Everybody Else,* addresses the idea of passion—this powerful, intrinsic, motivational force that drives the learner to pursue excellence. According to Colvin, the learner is compelled to go on chasing the dream that he or she envisions with every step closer to the ultimate goal. Yet passion is not given, it is bred within one, and it has a hold, a burning desire to continue the journey, no matter how difficult or how discouraging the moments may be. Passion imprints itself and invigorates constantly for the needed motivational thrust to keep going. Interestingly, extrinsic motivators, according to Coyle (2009), often lead to an unexpected outcome. Surprisingly, the more extrinsic the motivation, the more students become self-directed, setting their own goals and pushing themselves with intrinsic fuels. Isn't that ironic?

Gross motor movements motivate students, particularly with motivation that is totally invigorating and move the learner along at an accelerated pace of attentiveness. According to Willis (2010), this brain-friendly way to motivate students is through engagement. That tactic is easiest when the student is already active. That is to say, when the student is up and moving about, even if it is merely to gather supplies for the impending activity, the movement itself invigorates the system.

Movement causes oxygen to push into the brain and energize the mind as well as the body. Then it seems to be more conducive to getting students settled down with meaningful engagement in the task. This is a simple classroom tactic that may fly in the face of conventional classroom management wisdom. Often teachers have learned that students must not get into an activity until all directions have been stated. But movement seems to be a marvelous catalyst to authentic engagement with students and focused learning.

Finding ways to periodically invigorate to motivate the student already working hard, smart, and willingly, is still key to mounting the momentum needed for those final stretches that appear throughout their learning curve.

IMPACT

Whatever coaches or teachers can do to invigorate again and again must be used to optimize the learner's potential, provide some level of joyfulness in the journey, and provoke ongoing bursts of enthusiasm that fuel the learner. When this results in schools attending to invigorating lessons, units, events, and celebrations, when these behaviors become integral to the teaching and learning scene, schools on the brink of greatness will realize a highly motivated student body, poised and in position for developing the excellence these students are capable of demonstrating. This is the result of unlocking the talent within each learner.

Transforming Schools

The impact of this research on building greatness—developing expertise through practice, motivation, and coaching feedback—is not merely for a promising and talented few, but rather these are principles that can impact the learning experiences and expertise across the entire school population. It literally will change the culture of the school not only to one of high expectations, but to one that expects greatness in the face of all challenges.

Brief steps or methods to do regularly as part of classroom instruction include fostering aspirations through books, films, celebrations, and continued and progressively more challenging assignments, assessments, exhibitions, and competitions. It is also important not to overlook the influence that novelty of any kind has on learning, including all the effort, the fatigue, and yes, the "blood, sweat and tears" that go into that elite performer peaking.

Aspirations to Be Somebody

There really is nothing more invigorating for a developing talent to see in person, or in film, than their hero, their role model, or even a peer or competitor. It inspires, it invigorates, and it instills that desire for greatness even deeper into the soul of that being. After a ballet student was mesmerized by the stellar performance of the world's greatest ballet master, Mikhail Baryshnikov, as he danced and leaped and pirouetted across the stage, the young student left totally invigorated and went directly to the studio to try to imitate the elegant creature he had just seen.

It is so important to have that kind of eloquent models in the classroom for students to aspire to imitate. Examples include benchmarked papers of good, great, and exceptional essays or elegant math solutions depicted on graphing paper that can provide a vision and invigorate something inside the eager, aspiring learner.

Competiveness and Accomplishments

There is something about a competition that can light the fire of desire for excellence and a top-notch, personal-best performance. Even staging competitions in the classroom, with relays, enticing acknowledgments, and personal recognition, can cause students to rise to the occasion and get caught up in the moment of excitement and exertion. These are not uncommon strategies, yet the frequency of structuring these experiences seems to decrease with the increasing levels of schooling. Learning, practicing, and perfecting is fun, and it is part of the teachers' mission to make learning invitational and invigorating to foster excellence in all the kids.

Novelty Renews Commitment

Willis (2010) believes and practices with fidelity the principle that the emotional system must be tapped to get the learners' undivided attention. As we have said, Willis recommends novelty to arouse attention and curiosity to push the inquiry and investigation to pursue validation of the learners' thinking. In pursuit of this simple strategy that comes from tickling the natural curiosity of the human mind, she advocates a motivational, invigorating hook that causes the brain to go on alert.

Examples include anything that is surprising and novel—role-play in the classroom, a prop that catches their eye, a telltale sound that brings students to a point of focus, or even a guest or visitor appearing in the room at a designated moment. In short, get students excited, get them on your side, and you can teach them anything. Why? because, they want to learn it.

Hallmarks Celebrated

Excellent performance is a roller coaster of success and failure. And, in that very predictable process, it's just as important in the overall scheme of things to celebrate effort in as many ways as possible. That means celebrating the trials and errors as well as steps forward, acknowledging failures as steps clarifying the goal, and talking about how only those who have known failure and sensed the disappointment of losing can know the joy and empowerment of success. It takes all kinds of results to perfect the ultimate performance. Falling, stumbling, bungling a move are all familiar behaviors of the developing talent. It's all part and parcel of developing a champion.

PROFESSIONAL LEARNING COMMUNITIES DISCUSSION QUESTIONS

- Describe one instance when you have "invigorated" students with renewed energy, and their efforts have been beyond anything you had seen before.
- Reflect on how teachers can learn more about the power of motivational techniques to empower youngsters to excel. What kinds of classroom tactics invigorate their spirit to do their personal best?
- View a Judy Willis video online about the RAS (Reticular Activating System) to understand why "RAS Grabbers" are vital to get students' attention and sustain their curiosity.

PROFESSIONAL LEARNING EXERCISE: WHAT INVIGORATES YOU?

QUIZ: What invigorates you? Choose three and see what you know about you.

1. What movie? Explain.
2. What music? Describe.
3. What person? How?
4. What sport? Why?
5. What holiday? Justify.
6. What book? Tell more.
7. What chore? Seriously?
8. What place? Rationalize.
9. What pastime? Hmmm?
10. What possession? Qualify.

CHAPTER 3

Instill

Our best teachers do more than impart facts and figures—they inspire and encourage students and instill a true desire to learn. That's a fine art in itself.

—Sonny Perdue, Governor of Georgia (2003–2011)

A notable example of personal, internal, intense, and ever-present motivating passion instilled in a historic talent is the story of Ernest Hemingway and his urgency to do his writing, his pages, his word count, every single day. It was simply ingrained in how he lived his life, day by day, page by page, word by word. "Papa" Hemingway is said to have followed a routine in which he wrote 500 words a day and often did his writing standing up. Infused into his work were beliefs about the writing process itself (Hemingway, 1984). To understand the depth of expertise, Figure 3.1 gives the reader a window into the intensity of these instilled motivational machinations.

Revisiting the landscape of Part I, the three elements of motivation are separate and distinct, but they are also definitively interrelated. *Inspired* by moments of realization that a dream of greatness percolates, *invigorated* by a

Figure 3.1. Writing the Hemingway Way

1. To get started, write one true sentence . . .

The truest sentence you know.

2. Stop while you still know what happens next . . .

Stop when you're going good.

3. Never think about the story later . . .

You might lose the thing you were writing.

4. Always start by reading what you have written . . .

That's making it all one piece.

5. Don't describe an emotion—make it . . .

Identify action that caused the emotion.

6. Use a pencil . . .

To do this you have to work over what you write.

7. Be brief . . .

It wasn't by accident that the Gettysburg Address was so short.

growing labor of love as the automaticity of practice, repetition, and rehearsal energizes the mission, and *instilled* with a deep desire to conquer the goal brings the three motivational elements full circle. When people become entranced with the journey with their mind, body, and soul focused, alert, and on point, there is no turning back. The dream is alive and they have somehow instilled within themselves the complex blend of behaviors, attributes, and dispositions that will allow them to excel and eventually peak in their skillfulness as the expert.

Instill means "to put in place drop by drop; to gradually introduce, interject, infuse the confidence, spirit, and determination that signals those immersed in their vision to get the job done, whatever it takes." Their destinies are clear, their fates sealed. They are on their way to greatness.

INSTILLING THE WILL TO PREVAIL

Stepping back for a moment to put this phenomenon of talent unleashed into perspective, some of the theories and research, both qualitative and quantitative, target a singular, individual talent. Yet we believe, as most of our voices from the field suggest, that it is possible to take this to the academic arena to use with groups of students. Classrooms today seem ripe for corralling and applying the principles of developing the untapped talent, in classrooms, schools, and entire districts.

Figure 3.2. Motivation

To Instill a Growth Mindset
To Instill the Confidence of Know-how
To Instill the Sense of Fait Accompli
To Instill the Habit of Goal Setting
To Instill the Desire to Perform Above and Beyond
To Instill Pride and Uniqueness
To Instill the Need to Exceed, Give Back, Pay It Forward

Imagine if the ethos of the school was this: It's what you model, continually and with consistency, that becomes the new and elevated norm. It becomes the DNA of the school, and it is accepted that this is what we do, no questions asked. It becomes institutionalized in the policies and practices of the school. What if these three principles are ingrained, automatic and reflexive, as the school moves to these models of learning that put the students first? Could it, over time, become the signature piece of the school, the classes, the teachers, and the leaders?

While natural, innate talent does exist, developing talent needs enduring and nonstop nurturing to come to a full fruition. Talent is made, not born. A dynamic environment that instills these beliefs into the fabric of the school matters enormously. Jonathan Kozol (2007) believes that knowledge is passed on through instruction and imitation and that that is a testament to the cultural impact of a learning environment that values the untapped talents of each and every person. These are the bedrocks of developing potential and raising students to unknown heights, to unlocking the talent within.

Having said that, there are specific tactics that show promise in instilling the will to prevail. Acknowledging that each talent or performer is highly unique means that personalization of these strategies is a given. Conventional wisdom and dawning theories that seem to have remarkable promise for instilling the needed reserves for developing expertise or potential in students and classrooms of tomorrow are represented by seven interrelated dispositions. Each of the factors the authors have listed in Figure 3.2. is elaborated upon below, with examples that illustrate the concept and practical tactics to use in the classroom to instill these dispositions.

To Instill a Growth Mindset

A growth mindset (Dweck, 2006) affords the learner the liberty and reassurance to maintain a sense of self and a posture that embraces progress as well as success. A growth mindset rather than a fixed mindset accepts the possibility of failures as part and parcel of the learning curve. Learners that harbor a growth mindset understand the need to keep trying over and over again until they get it right, rather than telling themselves that they are failures and giving up or, even worse, never start that next challenge.

Serena Williams and her sister, Venus, were unlikely candidates for U.S. tennis championships. Despite their early long and arduous training regimens and their winning records on the teen circuit, they encountered criticism, doubt, and unfair prejudgment just as many of our students of color or foreign origins have experienced in school and elsewhere. The Williams sisters were subject to mistreatment by the media, fans, and even some of their colleagues. They just did not fit the image of tennis pros. Their body size and shape, their unconventional clothes, their unconventional journey with a Dad-coach, almost guaranteed a rough entry into the wide world of international tennis. Fortunately, both girls played so hard, so competitively, and so winningly, the tennis world had to respect their achievements. Even once they had the acknowledgment of their peers, who often lost matches to them, the critics held back the accolades until they finally, although not always as graciously as they could have, publically recognized both players as the elite players they had become. Despite everything, Serena and Venus had continued to believe in themselves. They had indeed marched ahead with their future visions, kept winning, achieving, and persevering. With all that it takes to stay on top, amazingly, at the same time, they created a successful fashion line of out-of-the-ordinary outfits that rankled the elite tennis crowd who wore white only on the courts . . . "white shorts and white shirts."

While both women continued to play in high-stakes tennis, Serena moved out and began a remarkable winning streak. In a nutshell, she ranked #1 in women's singles tennis on eight separate occasions to date. To be successful, to become the "winningest" female tennis star in the world, Serena had to find ways to instill an unwavering confidence in her ability, her drive, and her goals, to reach and remain on top.

Serena Williams (2015) tells the story about when she was competing for the 2008 U.S. Open Championship. She describes how she would collect matchbooks and write affirmations on them. During the match she would read them. It worked pretty well for her until she got an even better way to affirm herself and instill confidence and courage and creative energy. She came upon the idea of using her affirmations as her passwords, so that every time she signs in, she has an affirming message to fill her head with positives.

She revealed one affirmation she wrote once, "I will work in Africa and help kids and help people." And she did. She opened a school in Kenya in 2008 and another in 2010. Whatever determination she instilled in herself as an emerging, elite athlete, she apparently calls on at will, in all kinds of situations. She gets the job done in a big way. Period.

To Instill the Confidence of Know-how

A sense of ability and know-how parallels the move toward a growth mindset. Yet the student's acknowledgment of his ability and his understanding of the level of his know-how provide further self-assurance and a true sense of confidence in his own strengths. This is more than belief in one's self, this is about hard facts from a self-appraisal of one's skill levels. This self-knowledge instills a serious determination and helps set the learner's positive direction, leaving less room for doubt and second-guessing about his capabilities. This is an important component in developing excellence because learners at various stages in their training are sure to encounter setbacks, especially during practice days. One example of this is the known talent who develops a "trick" that showcases his or her extraordinary ability and know-how.

A young, amateur golfer, Taylor Laybourne, is featured on YouTube (B. Laybourne, 2016) picking up his club midswing, flipping the entire club upside down and hitting the ball squarely off the tee. He is a talented golf instructor and an aspiring Pro Tour candidate, demonstrating his own brand of skillfulness and confidence in a show-off way. But, still, it hints at talent instilled that exudes both playfulness and unwavering confidence.

To Instill the Sense of Will, Grit, Determination; a Fait Accompli

A. Duckworth (2016) has focused her studies on high performers and the sense of will, grit, and determination, even a feeling of fait accompli. These dispositions seem to fuel the obvious, ongoing development of expertise. As talent matures and moves through the progressive stages of excellence, if one can instill the feeling that it's going to happen, it's in the bag, then the will to finish is heightened and often conquered. If it's already completed in one's mind, that visualization can provide a magical moment.

Look at Lin-Manuel Miranda, a former high school English teacher, who always wanted to help students endure what they considered boring high school classes. Yet it wasn't until years later, in an exercise of grit, will, and determination, that Miranda was able to bring literature and history alive for students everywhere with his Tony-winning *Hamilton: An American Musical* based on Chernow's (2004) biography of Hamilton.

One can visualize the life of Alexander Hamilton and his contributions to the American story in starkly real terms. In fact, it has such an amazing impact on audiences, the demand for tickets is unimaginable. The PBS documentary (Horwitz, 2016) on Miranda's miracle Broadway musical provides a glimpse at Miranda's genius. Through will, determination, and raw grit, Miranda labored toward a final fruition of this project for 6 long years. The results show the perfection he demanded in his work.

To Instill the Habit of Goal Setting—and Goal Getting

Instilling a passion for goal setting and goal getting, which addresses the concept of "reachfulness" that both Coyle (2009) and A. Duckworth (2016) reference, seems to help create that burning desire to attain a personal best each and every time out of the gate. Setting goals is a learned skill that provides a step-by-step development toward greatness. Passion speaks to the love one has for what one is doing and is powered by the signs of a growing talent. The goals are just part of the built-in drive needed to attain such heights. Setting specific goals range from the perennial New Year's resolution to publically announcing a personal goal, to using fitness data to track health and fitness goals, to creating vision boards to imagine one's goals.

A remarkable example of the power of goal setting is illustrated dramatically by American swimmer Michael Phelps, the most decorated Olympian of all time with 28 medals from his remarkable time with the Olympic Games. At the 2016 Olympics in Rio, he worked his way through five competitions to win five gold medals, which was exactly the same number as his ambitious goal that drove him to these victories. (In fact, he won six medals, if you count the one silver medal he also won.) In his speech following the ceremonies, he stated that five medals had been his goal and he had achieved that, so he was satisfied and at age 31 was finally ready to call it quits (Park, 2016).

To Instill the Desire to Perform Above and Beyond

To instill the yearning for a performance above and beyond the status quo is sometimes what the elite learner lives for every day. It's a yearning that seems to accompany the passion one possesses for this highly personal mission. Walt Disney (JustDisney.com, 1998), even as a youngster, simply drew pictures all the time, anywhere and everywhere. He was naturally gifted and, as fortune would have it, somehow the environment he cultivated was brimming with art.

He was passionate about his art career and studied art and photography at McKinley High School in Chicago.School itself was not of much interest to him, except for creating cartoons, which were published in the school's newspaper. With hours and hours of drawing, his intrinsic motivation was present, yet there was an extrinsic motivation to make it materially rewarding. Young Walt traded his drawings to the local barber for free haircuts, and he would often sell drawings to neighbors to make extra money. He believed that once a person knew his passion, all his energy and talent needed to be funneled in that direction, and with enough effort he might actually achieve it. In his case he was right.

Walt Disney's legacy of animation and his many arenas of fantasy are the proof of his indomitable spirit, skill, and success. As an adult artist, he tells how Mickey Mouse just popped into his head one day. It was an image that was spontaneously there in his creatively gifted mind. He wanted to call him Mortimer, but his cohorts settled on Mickey. His ability to draw was not only always available to Walt, it was at the same time coached by this inner yearning to get his ideas on paper. He had to draw. It was what he did. When Disney's fourth animated feature film, *Dumbo,* premiered, Disney explained in an original interview with writer Ron Susskind that a simple story like Dumbo can still pack an emotional punch "because we all yearn to be part of the main, to be like everyone else." Yet, at the same time, we believe that we also want to be different enough to make our mark.

To parallel this extraordinary story of an American icon, there is another one of a young man currently in pursuit of his passion with performances above and beyond the norm. The yearning always resides deep within the person and seems to be present all of the time. Sean Nagata, as a toddler, was enamored by music and played piano with vigor and excitement. As a school-age youngster, he was plagued with learning difficulties and only seemed content when involved in some way with music.

That's when he started with the guitar. Eventually, he attended a college that accepted learning-challenged students, where Sean continued his passion for music. Once out of school entirely, he kept on with his music, now composing his own songs, writing lyrics and playing his songs whenever and wherever he could—family gatherings, friends' parties, neighborhood bars, in the park—practicing endlessly, anywhere and everywhere, with his guitar in hand, as he matured in his music, performances, and business acumen. He worked regularly as a street musician, throughout the subway matrix that stretches beneath the city of Chicago, to earn a living (www.youtube.com/watch?v=s-bULBEV2Vs). There he got lots of exposure and constantly got friendly, encouraging feedback. Fans started to follow him on his personally constructed website and he started to gain a steady following.

On his journey to become the best, he frequently organizes fellow musicians, comedians, and singers for local entertainment establishments and for the real audience experience that live performers need. He records his music on giveaway CDs and posts his original recordings on Facebook and YouTube. Sean plays wherever and whenever he can. He is traveling with the guitar, his constant companion, playing in Chicago, Honolulu, and in Freiburg, Germany. At last notice, he was off to the growing music scene in Berlin, hoping to continue to write, compose, perform, and network, possibly joining a band and recording his breakthrough album and hit song.

Sean is definitely intrinsically driven, always striving for the best he can do, seldom discouraged, but happy within this sphere of aspiring professionals. In fact, he is unwavering as his talent matures and he continues on the professional circuit of practices, rehearsals, presentations, and recordings, never flinching for one second that he may be mistaken about his talent and passion. He believes in his work, his talent, and his success. Not unlike others residing in our classrooms today, he has had a yearning for excellence and fame, and the recognition by his musician peers has grown with him over his 20-something years. This is a deep-seated feeling that may be known or unknown by other young people, and it supports them when teachers notice and help them advance their dreams in any way they can.

To Instill a Pride in Uniqueness

Instilling pride in the uniqueness of each performer is knowing and acknowledging that performers want to put their own mark on their performances, some kind of signature move or recognizable signal. These are manifestations of the pride that players have in their accomplishments, and it is one of the ways they begin to create their "brand." These are the signals of extraordinary performers that the general population recognizes instantly.

In fact, extreme talents, actors, athletes, artists, dancers, scholars, men and women, often are known for their adopted trademark of their excellence. Serena Williams's two-handed, backhand volley is copied incessantly by young players inspired by her astonishing skills on the court.

Our schools are full of youngsters who will benefit from our applications of the principles of internal motivators, yearnings to be great and the skill and will to practice and apply themselves in pursuit of expertise in their work, as well as with more lofty endeavors. We can instill these same instincts and desires to excel. Students are definitely likely candidates to respond to deep practice, motivational prompts, master coaching, and sometimes self-coaching just as superstars are.

To Instill the Need to Exceed, Give Back, Pay It Forward

The need to exceed is a phenomenon of the mentee, often surpassing the deeds of their predecessors in skillfulness and expertise. Outperforming previous contenders seems to be a motivating factor that drives talent to its peak. It's part of the phenomenon of the mentee exceeding the talents and skills of the mentor. Somehow, over time, the new talent ripens and often passes the mentor by breaking records and, more often than not, going on to develop a signature piece that puts them squarely in the limelight for the next generation of competitors. It's the cycle of progression that is as old as the hills, demonstrating the growing talent, enhanced by new methods of training, new rules, highly efficient equipment, and that ever-present, yet sometimes elusive, need to exceed, to give back or to pay back or even to pay it forward.

Examples abound in the field of figure skating. The triple salchows, double toe loops, triple axels, and other moves of the skaters at the 2014 Winter Olympics in Sochi, for example, were among some of the most stunning moments on ice. In 1976, 19-year-old Dorothy Hamill rose above expectations to win gold with her final skate in Innsbruck, Austria, ending the performance with her signature "Hamill Camel," a camel spin into a sit spin. In Tara Lipinski's 1998 free skate, her technically difficult performance included the famous triple loop–triple loop combination, fitting more spins into tighter, lower jumps. At the 1988 Winter Olympics, Brian Boitano landed eight triple jumps, including a Tano triple, and an impressive prolonged spread eagle for a nearly perfect performance that won him the gold medal. While similar findings are present in most sports, this small sampling shows what perfection for the experts requires of them—phenomenal accomplishment with feats of daring ("Ice-cool Plyuschenko," 2017).

VOICES

Ericsson and Pool

Ericsson and Pool (2016b) represent the concept of instilling determination as a maintaining and sustaining factor that may be what continually urges a talent to pursue every road leading to the ultimate reward. Their combined work on the absolute need for thousands of hours of practice surely must have an engine that can fire up, over and over again. It is this that they refer to as determination. They also believe that confidence comes with practice, repetition, and rehearsal; that work ethic, know-how, and expertise are empowering; and that there is nothing as motivational as instilling the self-direction to doggedly determine one's own path.

Duckworth

A. Duckworth (2016) discusses stamina, a stick-to-it-iveness, a deep commitment to the same area of achievement as grit. *Grit* is the ability to stay interested in things, and to get more interested in the same things. Duckworth sees no correlation between talent and grit, and has devoted her work to "super-high achievers." She influences the landscape with her discussions of "the plateau of arrested development" and the need for immediate, formative feedback that often seems to be lacking in education. In addition, Duckworth's notions about thousands of hours of practice parallel the concept of deliberate practice. Her thoughts on motivation lean toward the goal-setting model of "reachfulness" (Coyle, 2009), or in her words, "stretch goals."

Dweck

In the realm of motivating talent is Dweck's understanding of the influence others can have on a potential talent simply by using encouraging words, simple actions, subtle signals, and "Good Samaritan" deeds. Sometimes, the slightest comment, given at the right moment, stirs something in the inner psyche. It may not be explicitly noticed at the time, yet an awareness begins to grow when similar moments occur. These little stirrings seem to build to a point, which champion performers often comment on, the moment they realized that this is what they wanted to do.

IMPACT

In the introduction to this chapter on instilling motivational drive in emerging talents, the discussion focused on identifying and explaining a number of desirable dispositions extraordinary performers seem to possess and demonstrate throughout their journeys to that top slot. This discussion is geared to how these various aspects influence students, particularly in schools striving for excellence—schools marked by a culture that brings them to the brink of greatness. These cultivated behaviors can affect the turning points for teacher and student behaviors. There definitely are decision points that determine the growth and development of expertise, extraordinariness, and almost certain fame.

By fostering a growth mindset that affords the learner a sense of self and a posture that projects success, as well as a willingness to fail, students are more likely to feel fulfilled at school and in other life endeavors outside of school. School examples of well-known instances of a growth mindset are illustrated every day in our schools. When students try out for chorus or track or the debate team, they exhibit growth mindsets of confidence and risk taking. When they run for class president or student council, participate in the science fair, or submit an entry to the art exhibit, they manifest the positive qualities of a growth mindset. These are all examples of students willing to go through the trials and tribulations of competing or participating in high-stakes experiences, knowing that there are all kinds of possible outcomes. Yet they seem to know they have the resilience to bounce back, no matter what happens.

To develop growth mindsets, there are a number of strategies you can use when you know your students and when you use frequent, continual, and consistent feedback techniques. Try some of the suggestions given here in your classroom.

- **Know your students.** Probably the most fundamental and important element for teachers is to have a comprehensive knowledge and understanding of the students in their classroom in order to better accommodate student talents and needs. This might include readiness to learn, interests, and strengths and weakness, as well as social and emotional temperament and dispositions toward themselves and others. Teachers can direct students to online surveys to learn about themselves. Especially helpful are: interest inventories, multiple intelligences surveys, learning-style preferences, and tools to determine proclivities, talents, and raw abilities in problem solving and decision-making, art, music, drama, and computer technology.
- **Feedback techniques.** The close relationship with students links to the strategy for building a growth mindset through specific, immediate, actionable feedback for students. Teachers can offer feedback comments such as the following ones excerpted from Terri Eichholz's blog post (2016):
  » You never gave up.
  » You really improved on . . .
  » You have such a positive attitude.
  » That was a very responsible thing to do.
  » You're not afraid of a challenge.
  » What a creative way to solve a problem.
  » I can tell you studied hard because . . .
  » You worked well with your groups.
  » It was brave of you to . . .

Hattie's Feedback Techniques

In addition, Hattie (2012a), in "Feedback in Schools," spells out specific types of feedback that target student behaviors that answer three driving questions for students to consider:

Where am I going? (What are the goals?)
How am I going? (What progress is being made toward the goals?)
Where to next? (What activities need to be undertaken to make better
   progress?)

Hattie clarifies four feedback levels:

1. Feedback on task or product that is information focused (e.g., correct
   or incorrect)
2. Feedback on processes, formative and self-reference, rather than comparing to a norm
3. Feedback on self-regulation, "You're a little behind the pace that you
   need to get the writing done by Friday," indicating where students
   are, where they're going; monitoring learning
4. Feedback on the self that might sound like, "You are a great student,
   well done" (Hattie, 2012a).

To Instill a Sense of Know-How and Confidence

A sense of know-how tends to build confidence and self-assuredness, and
the learner harbors no doubt that he or she is capable. In a school setting,
this might be exemplified by the student who is willing to share the math
computation of a complex mathematical problem on the whiteboard for all
to witness. That student has the know-how and confidence.

Tomlinson's concept of knowing your students comprises students'
readiness, learning profile of strengths and weaknesses, as well as their hob-
bies, interests, pastimes, favorite sports, movies, music groups. In this way,
the teacher has a barometer to appraise the many dimensions of learners and
support their confidence.

To Instill a Sense of Will, a Feeling of Fait Accompli

To have this sense of will or actually be able to envision something complete,
is an affirmation for learners that it's going to happen, they will be able to
pull it off, and they have the actual wherewithal to execute what needs to
be done . . . it's going to happen. School examples involve systematic use
of "seeing in one's mind's eye" the performance successfully executed in
athletics, gymnastics, and diving. Teachers also use visualizations to rehearse
and instill determination and a sense of fait accompli to ease the stress and
pressure of high-stakes test taking. To introduce this tactic of learning how
to sustain the will and energy needed to complete tasks, simple visualization
exercises can help students.

In a life example, one professor would tell his weary doctoral students to see themselves walking across the stage to receive their degree. His advice was intended to instill the will to survive the grueling parts of the journey and to identify the needed perseverance and the plain old staying power that is so often needed.

Teachers can also ask kids to write their goals down, to make an oral commitment to a partner, to create a vision board or a collage depicting their dreams and aspirations fulfilled. In other tactics, teachers can provide a "Mirror, Mirror on the Wall Reflection Board," for students to post intermittent reflections. Another tactic that has been proven helpful for instilling the will to succeed is the use of benchmarked papers to illustrate a physical model of what an A paper (and B, C, and D papers) look like, or in essence, what success and failure look like.

To Instill the Yearning for Performance Above and Beyond Others

The yearning for performance above and beyond is also something that teachers can foster in the classroom. Students can develop a genuine yearning for personal academic success by exposure to many and varied examples of successful people in all walks of life. Colleges, careers, and job pathways must be shared, examined, and discussed to make options available to students who may not have developed their passion for even their possible field of interest yet. School-sponsored Career Days, inviting guest speakers, planning field trips for authentic learning experiences, and promoting role models from history as well as from current events can create excitement.

One glowing example that effectively makes kids astutely aware of ongoing schooling opportunities is the school building that has a huge college banner above each classroom door. Kids walking from class to class might be heard saying, "I'm going to Stanford." While they are really talking about a particular room in the building, just saying it can instill an aspiration and a belief in possibility. Curiosity is piqued, inquiries are made, and student expectations are clear. YOU are going to college. Where might you go? These are the kinds of cueing students may need to find their niche and to start thinking seriously about what their chosen path, their destiny, might be.

To Instill Pride in Uniqueness

This is about knowing how each elite performer makes his or her own personal mark on the performances; a signature move or recognizable signal that says "This is ME!" Somehow satisfying their need to leave an indelible mark becomes their personal and/or professional "Selfie." It is a highly individualized marker that is memorable for the feat or accomplishment that was performed. It's an affirmation of their talent, their development, and their unwavering effort to be the best they can possibly be.

School situations that mimic this effort to instill pride in students' work are fostered in self-directed efforts for perfection in classwork, in daily assignments and assessments and even in homework. Students also may show their pride in more subtle ways: always being the first to finish, selecting the most difficult library book, or even showing off their ability to share their expertise in math problems or digital challenges with another student. Teachers can also promote a healthy sense of pride by requiring students to graph their data and keep track of their personal bests in certain projects or performances; or by offering certificates for "personal best" work, certificates of achievement, or recognition through other means. For example, asking students to include evidence of three drafts, each showing improvement over the prior one, actually is a subtle maneuver on the part of the teacher to instill pride in the student's progress.

To Instill a Need to Succeed

The desire to succeed can be fostered in the K–12 classroom by arranging intermittent competitions that present a sense of urgency for a "personal best performance." One former colleague would hang a rope from ceiling to floor, displaying a sign that simply said "Spell-Wellers" for students to track their personal best scores on their weekly spelling test, by placing a clothespin at the appropriate height. No big deal, but it did create a buzz for a concerted effort by each student. Other ideas for instilling a need to succeed can be incentives for the entire classroom—popcorn day, movie time, or individual incentives such as five perfect math quizzes garners a "no homework day" or a day as "peer tutor" to help others.

PROFESSIONAL LEARNING COMMUNITIES DISCUSSION QUESTIONS:

- Write the sequence of a routine that is still in you, that was instilled in you years ago. Share the story of who and how.

- What trait is it your passionate mission to instill in your students each year? How do you go about the drip-by-drip, step-by-step, once-and-again-and-again process to know you have instilled this trait or idea or behavior?

- In terms of motivating youngsters with the yearnings for excellence, provide a quote, saying, proverb, or quip that captures the essence of what it means to instill something.

These suggestions for instilling determination to succeed and to excel can serve as platforms to be expanded as peers and colleagues share their ideas and strategies that work. Professional learning communities (PLCs) are structured to provide the time and place to converse about student talents and needs, to share instructional repertoires and possible interventions, to determine what is a next best step, and decide how that is going to happen.

PROFESSIONAL LEARNING EXERCISE: WHAT IS SPORTSMANSHIP?

Integrity Ranking Activity

Competition is a motivator, but students also need to learn the etiquette of competition behaviors. Think about the following scenarios and comment on each regarding fairness, integrity, and proper etiquette for amateur and professional participants.

1. The leading competitor exaggerates the number of her wins.
2. A runner-up, second-place winner, neglects to congratulate the winner.
3. Two winners, a tie. One congratulates the other. The other walks away without comment.
4. The predicted winner has a misfortunate misstep and is disqualified. She protests the call and plans to file a formal request for a change in the call.
5. An elite athlete is bombarded by fans and walks past the crowd with no acknowledgement.

Final Reflection: When is a lie a lie? What's your level of integrity? Rank the following types of lies as seen in Figure 3.3, each on a Rating of 1–10 (1 is lowest, 10 is highest).

Figure 3.3. Integrity Ranking Types of Lies

Assign a Ranking of 1–10 (10 is the worst) on the Likert Scale for each of the following situations. Then discuss highlights with your partner.

- Omitting information on a form
                    1   2   3   4   5   6   7   8   9   10
- Telling an outright falsehood to others
                    1   2   3   4   5   6   7   8   9   10
- Implying a mistruth to a family member
                    1   2   3   4   5   6   7   8   9   10
- Fibbing to a peer
                    1   2   3   4   5   6   7   8   9   10
- Telling a white lie to your parents
                    1   2   3   4   5   6   7   8   9   10
- Misrepresenting the truth to a friend
                    1   2   3   4   5   6   7   8   9   10
- Avoiding responding to an authority figure
                    1   2   3   4   5   6   7   8   9   10
- Lying on a legal document
                    1   2   3   4   5   6   7   8   9   10
- Not telling whole truth to an archenemy
                    1   2   3   4   5   6   7   8   9   10
- Exaggerating the truth to your sibling
                    1   2   3   4   5   6   7   8   9   10

Part I Classroom Teaching Ideas

What does motivation look like in the classroom? As teachers, we want to see and read about real examples of how teachers have integrated these critical skills of practice, motivation, and coaching feedback into their classroom.

With that in mind, there are examples at the elementary, middle, and high school levels for readers to consider, discuss, and adapt or try. Readers, leaders, and teachers can also share what they do to motivate and support social, emotional, and physical behaviors that foster the "untapped talent" of each student and to promote student success.

ELEMENTARY SCHOOL LEVEL: THINK, THEN ACT

Picture Book: *Wilbur Gordon McDonald Partridge* (Mem Fox, 1984/2017)

In this delightful tale of a young precocious boy who happens to live next door to a nursing home (Senior Center), his adventures are predicated by something he hears his parents say: "It's so sad, Miss Nancy is losing her memory." Now, Miss Nancy Allison Delacourt Cooper is his favorite resident because she has four names like he does. So Wilbur sets out to help Miss Nancy find her memory by asking everyone in the home what a memory is: It is something warm, it's something sad, it's something cherished. . . . Then he gathers a hen's egg that is warm, a picture of trapped animal, a high school golf trophy that is cherished and so on, and brings the basket to Miss Nancy. As she takes each item out, she tells a story of what it means to her . . . and "gets her memory back." Using this as an example, teachers can motivate students by teaching them about their own learning, their memories, and about how their brains work. In fact, there is a wonderful book called *It's All in Your Head: A Guide to Your Brilliant Brain* (2005) by Sylvia Funston and with vivid illustrations by Jay Ingram about the human brain and the cognitive mind. It leads easily into a conversation about how we forget because there is so much sensory input into the brain, and how we can learn to build our capacity for retaining memory. This is so important because memory is the only evidence we have of learning.

MIDDLE SCHOOL LEVEL: FINDING YOUR TRUE NORTH

Show a clip from the Warner Brothers film *Pay It Forward* (Leder, 2001), from the beginning to the part where the main character asks his students: "Is it possible for one idea to change the world?" He writes an inspirational challenge on the board:

> "Find something in this world you don't like, and do something about it."

Invite students to talk about the lack of direction and seemingly bored teens seen in the film. Then tell them that we can change ourselves, and the more we know about ourselves the more invigorating the assignment will be. Invigorate, energize, and tap the will to excel with "Flow."

Explain that Csikszentmihalyi's book, *Flow*, is all about that sense of pure enjoyment that one feels at times. As described in the title, *Flow: The Psychology of Optimal Experience*, "Flow" is total immersion of the person in a task with such intense focus, a sense of time that seems to fly by, and a self-awareness of total enjoyment in the moment, that the person is acutely aware of the feeling of joy (Pink, 2009, pp. 154–158).

One-Day Assignment: Set your hand-held alarm device to go off eight times during your waking hours that day. Each time the beep sounds, stop what you are doing and respond to these questions:

1. Which moments produced a feeling of "Flow"? Where were you? What were you working on? Who were you with?
2. At the end of the day, ask yourself: Are certain times of the day more "Flow"-friendly than others?
3. How might you increase the number of optimal experiences and reduce the moments when you felt disengaged or distracted?

After the self-survey investigation is over, debrief with general thoughts and reflections about optimal learning situations for different students.

HIGH SCHOOL LEVEL: ASK YOURSELF QUESTIONS

Ask Big Questions

Show a clip from Touchstone Pictures's *Dead Poets Society* (Weir, 1989). Begin with the part where Robin Williams is introducing the poetry text and is drawing a graph on the board. Then go to the scene where they are huddled together and he recites Whitman's "O Me, Oh Life" from *Leaves of Grass* (Whitman, 1891) and then addresses the boys: "'Life exists and identity/ That the powerful play goes on, and you may contribute a verse.' What will your verse be?"

Tell them the story of the advice that Clare Boothe Luce (quoted in Pink, 2009, p. 154) gave the young President John F. Kennedy: "A great man is one sentence. Lincoln freed the slaves. FDR lifted us from the Great Depression. What will your sentence be?"

Select one of the following to respond to:

- What will my sentence be?
- What will my verse be?
- What will be my legacy?

Then Keep Asking Small Questions

To realize your dream and aspiration takes much more than discovering your sentence. It takes lots of small steps and that means asking a lot of small questions along the way (Pink, 2009, p. 154). Am I on the right track? Is there a right way? Is there an easier way? Does this make sense? How long is it going to take? Are there shortcuts? How will I know it's right for me? Was I a little better today than yesterday? Give your students this list of questions and invite them to add others.

PRACTICING:
Engineer to Develop Expertise

Chapters in Part II offer the stage for an unusual read that gently contradicts much of what we know about motivation, practice, and coaching. Productive motivation for practice is not solely dependent on the internalized intrinsic motivation that has always risen above the external extrinsic brand, as illustrated in Part I. In Part II practice, as we know it, has morphed into a highly engineered skill, very different from the skill-and-drill we have learned and practiced and dreaded over the years. And coaching that is masterful seems a far stretch from the coaching feedback regularly, or maybe even periodically, given to our youngsters.

Repetitions (reps) are a commonly held protocol implemented for incremental and quality practice routines. However, as mentioned before, deliberate practice reps are engineered for developing expertise through multiple iterations using finely honed changes to produce continued, well-designed, and highly personal progressions.

Resistance and results are about working at the edge of one's ability and skill level. It's about practicing what one does not do well and requires extreme concentration, grit, and the guidance of the expert eye to coach for excellence in these fine-tuning exercises. It's about deep knowledge of the progressions within the skill development and the constant, specific, actionable feedback from the coach. Results are necessary and eagerly sought because of the intensity of this kind of deliberate practice. It's often performed in slow motion, with attention on the form and the function. Is it working? When it does, the results are the payoff for the work, for the supreme conscious awareness necessary to make the changes needed.

Recovery and residual create circumstances of the aftermath of intense exercise. Recovery is the resting period after the reach and repeat iterations and residual is the effect this deliberate practice has as it is being mapped in the mind. Instead of "more is better"—the common belief about practice— in deliberate practice the intensity and mental awareness, monitoring, and evaluating that accompany the carefully engineered iterations must be followed with a recovery period. While the practice itself is deliberately brief, the recovery benefits are well worth following the shortened daily routines used in this very different kind of practice. "Residual" references the mental models that develop in the brain/mind as the myelin continues to grow and wrap the axon of the neurons for the strength and speed needed for automaticity. That's how the gymnast, the skater, the diver, the golfer, and the student find the "sweet spot" time after time.

In sum, the process of deliberate practice embraces a marvelously effective routine called "reach and repeat." The continual stretching, reaching, earnest effort to surpass the previous record is what makes the determined mind that creates a personal best with each attempt.

CHAPTER 4

The Repetitions

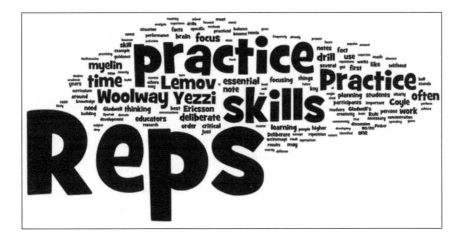

If people knew how hard I had to work to gain mastery, it would not seem so wonderful at all.

—Michelangelo

DELIBERATE PRACTICE

Deliberate practice: it's likely not what you think of when you hear the word *practice*. Noted researcher on the science of expertise, K. Anders Ericsson hails deliberate practice as "the most powerful approach to learning that has yet been discovered" (Ericsson & Pool, 2016b, p. xxiii). If this is the case, it is imperative that we come to understand what he means, but this will require letting go of some ideas about mere "practice" as we know it.

Malcom Gladwell's widely read book *Outliers* catapulted conversations about practice into the popular dialogue, particularly when he presented the "10,000 Hour Rule," claiming that this specific amount of practice was necessary to achieve eminence. There are, however, several problems with Gladwell's simplistic depiction of practice.

In all fairness to Gladwell, he has pointed out the nonacademic nature of his writings: "There is an important distinction to be made between popular works and academic works. My book is intended to be a popular work based on academic research, but it is not the same as an academic work. It is a different kind of literary enterprise. And it has to be judged by different criteria" (Gladwell cited in Gruber, 2006, p. 398). Our goals in this work are to accurately represent the scholarly research base and translate that for application by educators, so highlighting concerns around Gladwell's presentation of practice is warranted. With that said, and because more people have probably been exposed to Gladwell's book than to others cited here, Gladwell is revisited throughout the chapters to indicate his influence as one of the first messengers of this study to the public.

The first concern is that Gladwell framed his discussion around "The 10,000 Hour Rule." Gladwell credited Anders Ericsson, but Ericsson prefers conversations about extensive quantities of practice over years rather than a "rule" of a fixed amount, noting that in the case of young violinists, for example, "after only a few thousands of hours of solitary practice" they were "clearly superior to other groups of amateur musicians" (Ericsson, 2012). Yet, in other fields, due to the nature of competition and refinement of training, 10,000 hours would not nearly be sufficient to perform on a world-class level.

More critically, Gladwell's conversations about practice did not explore an important element. Gladwell merely discusses "practice" without a modifier. Ericsson and many others discuss "*deliberate* practice" and Coyle (2009) discusses "*deep* practice." We have chosen to use the term "deliberate practice" as it is most consistently used in the literature. Regardless of the modifier used, as Colvin (2008) remarks, deliberate practice "isn't what most of us do when we're 'practicing,'" directly acknowledging that deliberate practice is something well beyond typical practice.

Myelin

The brain really is like a muscle. In fact, brain development through practice holds much in common with developing muscles. The brain develops through sensory input received by dendrites, which are a part of the neuron or brain cell. In turn, when the brain is learning, messages are sent out through the axon. The more frequently the neurons send messages, the more the myelin wraps around the axon. The more repetitions, the more myelin is generated, which in turn continues to strengthen the connections.

As noted earlier, the new information on how myelin develops suggests that, although we tend to starkly delineate between the physical and the cognitive, the dynamics of practice seem quite parallel across both physical and cognitive endeavors. Exploring deliberate practice through a gym-based analogy works quite well, and the instructional practices of great teachers often share much in common with great coaching. Thus, this text frequently references teacher/coach synonymously and a workout-based metaphor will continue to unfold.

The Myelin-building

The first message of myelin is one of repetition. The only way to build up the myelin needed to optimally insulate a neural circuit is to repeatedly fire that circuit through ongoing practice. This physiological perspective explains why new skills are difficult for us all as we begin. We have no myelin along the accompanying neural pathways. The necessary impulses are traveling slowly and the refractory time (time between signals) is significant. As a result, undertaking the activity requires more concentration.

Consider an elementary school student just learning single digit multiplication. The multiples of some numbers, 2 and 11 for example, come fairly easily, but others, like 7, require far more effort and concentration. When the teacher asks the class, "What is 6 x 7?" several seconds elapse before someone sheepishly volunteers "42," not completely sure that the answer is correct. Then skip ahead several years to a middle school classroom where every student is working a math problem involving the multiplication of 6 and 7. The answer to that element, 42, instantly comes to mind with almost no conscious thought. Myelin has grown. Skill and speed are now present.

As Coyle (2009) notes there is no shortcut to building myelin; you cannot take a pill to accelerate its development. Even the most casual gym-goer knows that if you want to get results, the first step is actually exercising. Simply being active and moving brings results, and every repetition of a skill brings us a bit more myelin.

> As noted there is no shortcut to building myelin. You cannot take a pill to accelerate its development.

The 80/20 Rule

Once we understand the quantity of repetitions necessary to build skills, essential considerations become *which* skills to practice and *how* to best go about practicing them. If effective practice requires hours of repetitions, how do you decide where to focus when you already have more to do than you reasonably can? Educators frequently and rightfully bemoan the fact that there are often far too many things that they are required to teach than they reasonably can, resulting in a "mile wide, inch deep" dilemma. How is this reality reconciled with the dynamics of practice?

In resolving this tension, Lemov et al. (2012) suggest guidance from "The 80/20 Rule" or "law of the vital few." They note that this is "a pattern that holds true again and again: 80% of results come from 20% of the knowledge acquired or skills developed within a domain" (p. 29). In essence, then, each subject area likely contains an essential 20% that ultimately accounts for 80% of our success or performance in that domain. As a result, Lemov et al. (2012) suggest that educators thoughtfully identify and focus practice on "the 20 percent of things that most create value" more intently "than the other 80 percent of things [they] could plausibly spend time on" (p. 29).

We can easily apply this idea in mathematics. Basic math facts (key operations within Base 10) would clearly qualify as part of the "20%" or "vital few." When key math facts are well known, all other topics in mathematics are facilitated. When they have not been mastered, everything else is encumbered.

As MIT professor Stephen Pinker (1997) notes, "Math is ruthlessly cumulative." While we consistently acknowledge this when focusing on basic arithmetic operations or "math facts," "calculus teachers lament that students find the subject difficult not because derivatives and integrals are abstruse concepts—they're just rate and accumulation—but because you can't do calculus unless algebraic operations are second nature and most students enter the course without having learned the algebra properly and need to concentrate every drop of mental energy on that." In other words, they have not sufficiently practiced the algebra skills to build myelin.

Portions of the overall 20% are scattered throughout all levels of the content, but some educators resist focusing on particular, isolated skills intensely, particularly when this might be viewed as "low-level repetition." Similar to the earlier observation of Lemov et al., Pinker (1997) notes a problem in that "drill and practice, the routes to automaticity" are, by some, undervalued and put down as "'mechanistic' and seen as detrimental to understanding." He notes that "the way to get to mathematical competence is similar to the way to get to Carnegie Hall: practice." Would a world-class violinist tell someone that the scales they have continually practiced over the years were of no benefit? When skills are essential, sufficient, sustained practice is justified.

Identifying the 20%

So, how do educators determine which are the most essential skills? The concept of the "vital few" is not completely foreign to educators who may already have had discussions about the "non-negotiables" or "power standards." We have intuitively known that not all skills are created equal, but we often fail to consistently use that knowledge in our planning and prioritization.

In some cases, existing curriculum documents may provide guidance in seeking to identify this critical 20%. When these are not present, Lemov et al. (2012) suggest, it is often the case that teachers "may know these things already from experience" (p. 30). These authors also point out that, when no other guidance is available, we can "consider harnessing the wisdom of crowds" by "[assembling] a group of relatively informed people and [asking] them to name" the most important skills. They note that "aggregating the opinions of multiple people often yields an accurate analysis of a tough situation" (p. 31).

> We have intuitively known that not all skills are created equal, but we often fail to consistently use that knowledge in our planning and prioritization.

The 20% May Be More Like 30%

Finally, work in the emerging area of learning progressions often includes the identification of essential skills that become strong prerequisites for subsequent ones, sometimes referred to as "focus skills."

Consider work done by the National Foundation for Educational Research (NFER) in developing a learning progression for the national curriculum of England as profiled in Kirkup, Jones, Everett, Stacey, and Pope (2014). They offered a definition of *focus skills* as those "that are essential to progression, that support the development of other skills in the same or future years and/or are central to the emphases of the [particular curriculum]" and note that "these skills constitute the areas that pupils need to master in order to become successful" with the subject (p. 9).

Their detailed analysis of the entire mathematics curriculum in England revealed 1,000 specific teachable skills across all years of school. Of these 1,000 skills, 30% were identified as focus skills, and 42% of all focus skills were found in the "number and place value" domain. In reading, slightly over 1,100 overall skills were identified, with 29% of those being noted as focus skills. The majority of the focus skills (61%) were found in the "word reading" domain, which deals with phonics knowledge and skills, word recognition, and fluency.

Knowledge of focus skills drawn from such sources can be extremely useful in planning. As Popham (2007) notes "identifying 'must-learn' building blocks enables teachers to plan instructional sequences that give students systematic rather than sporadic opportunities to master each building block in the learning" (p. 83).

Disproportionate Practice

Once the 20% of critical skills is identified, we must then allocate a disproportionately favorable amount of time to them. Lemov et al. (2012) note that "if you're practicing one of those important skills—one of the 20% of skills that drive 80% of performance—don't stop when your participants 'know how to do it' . . . [because] your goal with these 20-percent skills is excellence, not mere proficiency" (p. 30). *Automaticity, fluidity,* and *fluency* are also terms that surface in these discussions. The goal "is to be great at the most important things" (p. 31).

> Popham notes "identifying 'must-learn' building blocks enables teachers to plan instructional sequences that give students systematic rather than sporadic opportunities to master each building block in the learning" (p. 83).

Lemov et al. (2012) remark that because you will now be spending more time doing more practice with the 20%, "the 80/20 rules will likely cause you to spend more time planning" in the short term because "you have to design extremely high-quality activities for your 20-percenters" (p. 32). However, "once you've done that, you'll no longer waste time preparing a smorgasbord of activities you'll use briefly and discard. You invest in developing better activities that you will use over and over" (p. 32).

Higher Order Thinking

The role of practice in fostering creative and higher order thinking must be considered. At the same time that practice has been characterized as low level, educators have sought to foster creativity and higher order thinking by planning extensive, open-ended explorations. While these are clearly needed in an appropriate quantity and at key points during instruction, Lemov et al. (2012) note that we may be tempted to rush through practice on the basics to get to greater depth when, in fact, we can often "unlock creativity, with repetition." They note that "creativity often comes about because the mind has been set free in new and heretofore encumbered situations" (p. 38).

Think about your own experience. When do your best ideas come to you? It's typically in one of two situations. Sometimes it is when we are engaged in routine activities that we have rather automated—taking a shower or cutting the grass. Since our brains are continually active, in situations where little processing power is required for the basic task at hand they often redirect their surplus capacity to other tasks.

Other times our best ideas come when we understand the underlying basics extremely well. We have automated them. We have myelinated them.

Students are unable to connect high-level ideas within or across domains when they do not understand well the basics of those domains.

While anything can be overdone and we clearly need a balance between working with the basics and then applying them in deep and open-ended ways, spending time focusing on basic facts and operations need not be "characterize[d] with the pejorative 'drill and kill'" or considered "the enemy of higher order thinking" as, "it's all but impossible to have higher order thinking without strongly established skills and lots of knowledge of facts" (Lemov et al., 2012, p. 37). We need balance.

ACHIEVING BALANCE: DRILL VERSUS SCRIMMAGE

In striving to help educators achieve an appropriate balance between focusing on essential skills and helping students apply concepts deeply, Lemov et al. (2012) draw from sports vernacular and present the concepts of drill and practice for use in planning.

Drill to Learn

Drilling is often a purposeful and appropriate instruction choice because "a drill deliberately distorts the setting in which participants will ultimately perform in order to focus on a specific skill under maximum concentration to refine that skill intentionally" (Lemov et al., 2012, p. 48). This is not unlike Ericsson, Krampe, and Tesch-Römer's (1993) discussion that "deliberate practice would allow for repeated experiences in which the individual can attend to critical aspects of the situation and incrementally improve her or his performance in response to knowledge of results, feedback, or both from a teacher" (p. 368). Deliberate practice discussions note that world-class experts routinely drill by focusing intently on one specific aspect of performance.

It is only during such a time of intent focus that individual skills can be refined, practiced with precision, and mindfully repeated to allow myelin to strategically develop. Coyle observed focused drilling at Spartak Tennis Club in Moscow, one of the world's most successful tennis schools. Practice there often does not involve a ball, and sometimes does not involve a racket. They refuse to rush a novice tennis player into a game situation without having first repeatedly practiced each key skill while focusing and repeating the motions slowly and then subsequently building speed.

"At Spartak it's called imitatsiya—rallying in slow motion with an imaginary ball" through focused drills of "slow, simple, precise motions with an emphasis on tekhnika—technique, " Coyle (2009) notes and points out that "all [of] Spartak's players do it, from the five-year-olds to the pros" (p. 82).

Famed UCLA basketball coach John Wooden did the same thing. He often had players practice without the ball. He noted that the ball was a "distraction caused by the player's natural instinct and desire to score baskets and grab rebounds," which makes it hard for them to "pay attention and learn the 'dull' fundamentals that ensure success" (Wooden & Jamison, 2005, as quoted in Coyle, 2009). The strategies at booth Spartak and UCLA seem to mirror this drill concept of intensely focused practice—distorting the situation so as to achieve maximum concentration on key skills. Similarly, a teacher might have students undertake a "focused revision" of a paper by reviewing the work for one key element only. Students would be told to revise that and only that element, ignoring other elements of the work. This direction helps students "drill" on that skill/element by focusing them intently on that aspect.

Scrimmage to Apply

"A scrimmage, by contrast, is designed not to distort the game (like drills) but to replicate its complexity and uncertainty," say Lemov et al., (2012). These situations are critical as "success in scrimmage is the best indicator of true mastery" and are needed to ensure that "participants can perform a skill when the time and place of its application is unpredictable" (p. 50). The full paper or project is a scrimmage. It could also be a group of students practicing their team presentation or a debate.

There is, however, a paradox within the drill–scrimmage relationship. Despite the fact that scrimmages are "the best indicator of true mastery," "scrimmaging is generally less efficient *as a teaching tool* [emphasis added]" (Lemov et al., 2012, pp. 50–51). It is during the drill when most learning, most acquisition of skills, occurs.

> It is during the drill when most learning, most acquisition of skills, occurs.

Additionally, it is critical that the drill-scrimmage relationship not be viewed as a stark dichotomy. While some "believe that scrimmage is the only way to teach participants to integrate skills, drill can easily integrate skills." Understanding how to arrange these various forms of practice (see Figure 4.1) for learners represents the orchestration of "graduated practice," which, according to Lemov et al. (2012) "is what sets the champion coaches in all fields apart from the merely good" (p. 51). The continuum, then, becomes single skill drills, multi-skill drills, and scrimmages all orchestrated by a master coach, with the result being preparation for the "championship game," which might be high-stakes exams or postsecondary endeavors.

Figure 4.1. Repetitions: The Progression from Practice to Mastery

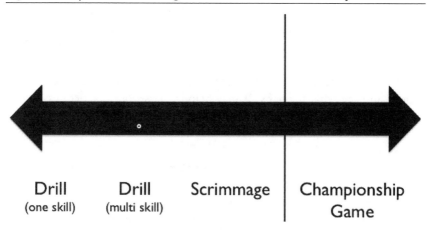

| Drill | Drill | Scrimmage | Championship |
| (one skill) | (multi skill) | | Game |

This, however, is just the first necessary consideration. Repetitions merely equate to practice, and the science of expertise focuses on "deliberate practice." Other elements must be considered to further delineate deliberate practice, and these elements are the subject of the next chapters.

PROFESSIONAL LEARNING COMMUNITIES DISCUSSION QUESTIONS

- What's your reaction to Lemov et al.'s 80/20 Rule? How might you apply this individually and as a team? Is this a concept that you might share with students, and to what benefit?
- What guidance do you have, or need, to determine the essential skills and content you must teach?
- What insights did the "drill versus scrimmage" discussion provide for you as you consider planning practice? Do you feel you are in balance?
- What do you feel is the relationship between practice and creativity?

PROFESSIONAL LEARNING EXERCISE: STRINGING SKILLS

The concept of combining, or stringing together, a series of skills to create a higher order or more complex practice of drill skills parallels a similar innovation described in *Making Thinking Visible* (Ritchart, Church, & Morrison, 2011). In that book the students are linking thinking skills into a chain that hangs together in a "thinking routine." Ritchart et al. give examples of thinking categories with several routines in each: Exploring includes the routines of See–Think–Wonder and 3,2,1 Bridge; Synthesizing includes Color–Symbol–Image; Digging Deeper includes Claim, Support, Question.

Develop a practice that strings several skills you use all the time: Lessons with Plan–Teach–Assess or Writing with Draft–Read–Edit. It might be best to have participants work in small groups and develop their "Chain Practice" that combines three skills you frequently used when doing a more robust project and see what happens. It may help in classroom practice sessions to think about stringing the skills.

LEARNING MORE

Deliberate Practice and the Science of Expertise—*The Talent Code* by Dan Coyle (2009) provides a wonderful summary of research coupled with illustrative examples from Coyle's multiyear analysis of "hotbeds of talent." K. Anders Ericsson and Robert Pool's (2007) *Peak: Secrets from the New Science of Expertise* is extensively cited by all others in the field. Though written for business leaders, the majority of the Geoff Colvin's (2008) *Talent is Overrated: What Really Separates World-class Performers from Everybody Else* is applicable to broad audiences, and his introductory narrative where he debunks the myths of talent around Mozart and Tiger Woods is illuminating. Finally, *Bounce: The Myth of Talent and the Power of Practice*, written by British table tennis star Matthew Syed (2011), is another excellent general source.

CHAPTER 5

Resistance and Results

Never mistake activity for achievement.

—John Wooden

When discussing the repetitions that deliberate practice requires, we are peering into the brain to observe the physiological changes (building up of myelin) that result from practice. We can document these changes through brain imaging, and the knowledge of this physiological process has clear implications for instructional planning—we must make time for the necessary repetitions. However, to further study deliberate practice, we begin explorations that are not easily seen, like the inside of a black box. We will not be able to perceive everything clearly, but based on years of observation and study by Ericsson and others, researchers in the field have all developed, supported, and advanced several key hypotheses.

Is Practice Worthy of Precise Engineering?

In order for us to fully operationalize the new insights from the science of expertise on optimal skill acquisition, some deprogramming may be necessary.

This is due to the fact that practice has sometimes been thought of as basic or low-level. According to Lemov et al. (2012), "the underestimated concept of practice" has often been "seen as mundane and humdrum, poorly used or much maligned, or too familiar to be interesting" (p. xvii). They note that "practice is often considered unworthy of deep, sustained reflection and precise engineering" (p. xvii), yet, according to expert research, nothing could be further from the truth. Precise engineering is required and it goes well beyond making the time for repetitions.

The late UCLA basketball coach John Wooden clearly believed that practice was worthy of precise engineering. Former players always note the intensity of Wooden's practices that were "the product of extensive, detailed, and daily planning based on continuous evaluation of individual and team performance" (Gallimore & Tharp, 2004, p. 124). It is reported that Wooden spent 2 hours every morning with his assistant coaches planning practices that might have lasted less than that amount of time, and he "kept a record of every practice session . . . for future reference" (Gallimore & Tharp, 2004, p. 125).

But it is not just about planning activities. As John Wooden once remarked, "Bustling bodies making noise can be deceptive" (quoted in Lemov et al., 2012, p. 21). "Hustle and bustle can distract us from noticing when we're not actually that productive" (Lemov et al., 2012, p. 22). We can remain quite active practicing things, while never moving into a zone of deliberate practice. How do we make our practice the most effective it can be?

> "Hustle and bustle can distract us from noticing when we're not actually that productive.

Turning Hustle and Bustle Into Deliberate Practice

Ericsson, Krampe, and Tesch-Römer (1993) present deliberate practice as "activities that have been specially designed to improve the current level of performance" and that are crafted in consideration of the following:

1. The design of the task should take into account the preexisting knowledge of the learners so that the task can be correctly understood after a brief period of instruction.
2. The subjects should receive immediate informative feedback and knowledge of results of their performance.
3. The subjects should repeatedly perform the same or similar tasks. (p. 368)

In their criteria, you can clearly see a consideration of the repetitions needed to build myelin, but those are only undertaken once a specific activity has been planned in relation to the learner's current level—*resistance*—and feedback on performance—*results*—is given. In this chapter we explore these additional aspects of practice: resistance and results.

RESISTANCE EXTENDS PRACTICE POTENTIAL

Are you operating on the edge? Resistance is the next element that delineates the deliberate practice that maximally develops expertise even further from mere practice. To optimally develop skill, appropriate resistance, reach, or stretch must be considered. Observational research and instructional theory suggest that when we are operating on the edge of our abilities, we grow the most.

Coyle (2009) illustrates the concept by providing lists of related works in two formats. In the first format, two related words are written out fully (e.g., pen / paper). In the second format, a single letter is omitted from each word (e.g., m_lk / cere_l). According to Coyle, studies have shown that people remember more—up to three times more—from a list where blanks are inserted into the words. He asserts that when encountering the blanks, "you stopped . . . you stumbled ever so briefly, then figured it out . . . you experienced a microsecond of struggle, and that microsecond made all the difference" in terms of retaining the information (p. 17).

This is not unlike Russian psychologist Lev Vygotsky's (1978) well-known concept of the "zone of proximal development [ZPD]," which he defined as "the distance between the actual developmental level . . . and the level of potential development . . . under adult guidance, or in collaboration with more capable peers" (p. 86). In short, if we are not pushed or stretched, we do not grow. If we are pushed too much, we become overly frustrated. But if we are pushed at an ideal level—just beyond our reach—we grow optimally.

Though developed in different ways and from different perspectives, deliberate practice as described by the science of expertise and Vygotsky's zone of proximal development share many common elements. While the concept of ZPD is familiar to many educators, most of us have merely accepted it at a very basic level, failing to deeply and regularly reflect on what it means and its full implications for planning instruction. We understand the concept, but does it really guide our daily planning? Likely not. But it should. By exploring deliberate practice, we are actually deepening our understanding of ZPD in meaningful ways.

Vygotsky's conversations compared developing skills to fruit growing on a vine. He felt that when students work within their ZPDs, the "ripening" of their skills was accelerated. He remarked that "the only good kind of instruction is that which marches ahead of development and leads it: it must be aimed not so much at the ripe as the ripening functions" (Vygotsky, 1986, p. 188). Focusing on skills that are not "ripe," however, can require immense energy.

The Challenges of Applying ZPD

Teachers face several challenges in planning instruction through a ZPD mindset. First, the ZPD is never the same for all students in any class. While teachers can gauge a median ZPD of a whole class—shooting to the middle—the real power, and challenge, of ZPD is in differentiating for groups and individuals whose ZPDs differ. In this sense, ZPD is merely one more of the chorus of requests that asks us to work toward more targeted or personalized delivery of instruction. Working to more directly target instruction through flexible skills groups takes additional planning and coordination, but it also creates a dynamic that places more students in their ZPDs.

ZPD: A Moving Target

Teachers must also "realize that the zone of proximal development is a moving target" because "as a learner gains new skills and abilities, this zone moves progressively forward" (Cherry, 2016). The challenge of keeping students working within their zones of proximal development is a significant and never-ending one. Managing this challenge can be greatly aided through the adept use of formative classroom assessment strategies, which we will discuss later. These strategies can provide a continuous flow of information—feedback—to both teachers and students on how they are performing.

Embracing the Struggle

Finally, the appropriate zone for optimal practice is not only challenging for teachers to continually create, it can also be hard for students to endure. We must acknowledge that we learn best when we struggle appropriately. But appropriate struggle is a fine line to walk continually—as the world's experts do.

Based on surveys from popular activities such as golf and tennis, Ericsson and Charness (1994) find that "the vast majority of active individuals spend very little if any time on deliberate practice. Once amateurs have attained an acceptable level of performance, their primary goal becomes inherent enjoyment of the activity, and most of their time is spent on playful interaction" (p. 734).

Deliberate practice is very different from "playful interaction." It entails considerable, specific, and sustained efforts to do something you can't do well—or even at all" (Ericsson, Prietula, & Cokely, 2007, pg. 117). It "involves constantly pushing oneself beyond one's comfort zone" (Ericsson & Pool, 2016b, p. 17). Observations of the world's experts in various fields reveal that they strive to work continually within this uncomfortable zone that so many of us, including our students, seek to avoid. Coyle advises teachers and students to "embrace struggle and repetition" but notes that, typically, "kids don't embrace either and we (as teachers) don't embrace repetition" (Coyle, personal communication, 2011).

Helping Students Endure Deliberate Practice

Perhaps one of the first ideas to convey to students is that to grow optimally, they must learn to "practice like the experts." Videos, stories, and examples of successful individuals, profiling how they targeted areas of their performance to improve and then undertook deliberate practice in those areas, could be powerful motivators.

We might also stress that practicing alone is one thing, and practicing with the assistance of others is something else. Vygotsky (1978) stressed that the challenge of the ZPD required that students work "under adult guidance, or in collaboration with more capable peers" (p. 86). Working in the zone is tough. With support, the work is optimal. Without the support of peers or adults, the work can be overwhelming. The challenge is for teachers to support students who are in many different zones. To do this they might consider regular opportunities for group work and peer interaction, both of which have well-documented positive effects (Schacter, 2000; Slavin, 1995).

Ultimately, Vygotsky viewed learning as a very social endeavor, noting the power of social interactions to support students operating on their edges of performance—clearly something to think about in relation to deliberate practice and planning.

When discussions of ZPD are considered alongside ones of deliberate practice, there is a feeling that deliberate practice is on the extreme upper ends of ZPD and that the most successful individuals are more willing to continually engage is daunting activities than many of us. As Syed (2011) notes, "The paradox of excellence is that it is built upon the foundations of necessary failure" because "excellence is about striving for what is just out of reach," "grappling with tasks just beyond current limitations," which can result in "falling short again and again" (p. 120). When we can tolerate this challenging place where we continually grapple, something almost magical begins to happen. Students want to learn, and if we can give them this experience of seeing failure and challenge as steps toward success, they will be nourished for future efforts over a lifetime.

RESULTS INSPIRE AND INFORM PRACTICE

Ericsson, Krampe, and Tesch-Römer (1993) note that "deliberate practice requires effort and is not inherently enjoyable" (p. 391). Very few are willing to push themselves to do the massive amounts of deliberate practice that expertise requires. It is tough work. How, then, are teachers to use this new knowledge to improve learning? How can they help their students embrace the struggle that most of us so quickly seek to avoid?

Though not inherently enjoyable, deliberate practice can be varied in form so as to be more novel to the learner. Working in a group can be engaging, as can competition or public exhibitions. These, however, will only provide a bit more motivation. To create a motivational force that can continually drive efforts, our focus must be fundamentally shifted from how challenging the work is to something else.

Daily reaching and struggling to grow skills and abilities can be enjoyable, but only if one receives continual feedback noting this growth. We see this as many people undertaking physical training are driven by their tracking devices (e.g., Fitbit) to work daily toward goals. Feedback is the key. It's the monitor on the treadmill, the ball that goes in the basket, or the muscle and definition that builds slowly after workouts. The challenge with academic pursuits, however, is that growth or progress in them is often much harder to perceive than on a sports field or in a music or art class.

> Daily reaching and struggling to grow skills and abilities can be enjoyable, but only if one receives continual feedback noting this growth.

How often do students feel that they are working hard without a sense of growing or making any progress? Some teachers may remark that certain students appear lazy or do not put forth effort, but those same students will spend hours undertaking work where their results are more tangible. Are they lazy? Or are they frustrated from trying and not feeling like they are going anywhere? How do we make the growth in academic pursuits as visible or tangible as the swish of a basketball hitting nothing but net? How might we use feedback to drive that learner?

Because deliberate practice is so challenging, feedback on success—the results—becomes a critical element for multiple reasons. As noted, feedback can be extremely motivating. Ericsson, Krampe, and Tesch-Römer (1993) note that with feedback "individuals are motivated to practice because practice improves performance" (p. 368), not because the deliberate practice is enjoyable. They clearly state that "in the absence of adequate feedback, efficient learning is impossible and improvement only minimal even for highly motivated subjects" (Ericsson, Krampe, & Tesch-Römer, 1993, p. 367).

Beyond the motivational aspects of feedback, the specific results from practice are immediately needed so that both the learner and the coach can determine whether the targeted skill was practiced correctly and use that information to inform future practice. Given that deliberate practice requires focusing on the edge of our abilities, immediate feedback is even more critical. If we are focusing on the edge, we are far more likely to make mistakes. Information from these mistakes can be used for our betterment or ignored to our detriment.

It is essential that we (both students and teachers) know when things are not being practiced correctly so that corrections can be made as soon as possible. This is critical because the brain will myelinate incorrect behaviors just as quickly as correct ones. Every repetition performed correctly deposits a bit of myelin that builds skills, but every repetition performed incorrectly deposits a bit of myelin that cements misperceptions or incorrect behaviors.

Unlearning

When something has been learned incorrectly, we have literally created a neural pathway to support incorrect behavior. Unlearning is harder than learning. To overcome an incorrectly learned skill takes much more effort. When the learner is made aware that he or she is performing something incorrectly, it requires intense focus to perform the skill correctly, and this level of attention must be maintained during subsequent practice until a new neural pathway at least as robust as the initial incorrect one is formed. This is exemplified when you switch from pedal brakes to hand brakes on a bicycle. Many of us pressed the pedal for quite a while on our new ten-speeds with hand brakes.

Consider an example given by Lemov et al. (2012) of a youth sports practice in light of Ericsson, Krampe, and Tesch-Römer's criteria for deliberate practice. Two soccer coaches set up four activities for their players to rotate through. While these activities may have been planned based on pre-existing knowledge and skills, with four simultaneous activities and only two coaches, dynamics are created where many players rotate through stations and practice skills without immediate feedback. This creates a situation where practice potentially becomes detrimental.

Without feedback, students likely should not repeatedly perform the same or similar task. The longer the practice continues without feedback, the greater the possibility that skills are being myelinated incorrectly. An immediate implication for teachers is to have their students practice only what they can easily observe, either directly or indirectly, or at least be concerned when prolonged practice without observation or assessment has occurred.

Flipped Classrooms

This emphasis on closely monitored practice fits well with the current interest in "flipped" classrooms. Within this strategy significant parts of instruction are flipped to become at-home activities. For example, many math teachers now have students watch Khan Academy videos or teacher-created videos as instructional homework in preparation for additional instruction and monitored practice in class the next day. Historically, practice was accomplished through homework and thereby was undertaken without the teacher's supervision. Within this model, practice occurs in the classroom under the teacher's watchful eyes.

What Forms Should Results Take?

Reframing the importance of feedback in terms of motivation is one thing. Understanding what forms feedback should take—how and when to present it—is quite another, and our record in giving effective feedback in education is not stellar. To be clear, we give a lot of feedback. The problem is that, often, that feedback makes little to no positive impact on learning.

One of the most comprehensive reviews of research on feedback is Kluger and DeNisi's 1996 meta-analysis. In this comprehensive work, they reviewed over 3,000 studies related to feedback ranging as far back as 1905. Once filtered for rigid design and broadly generalizable results, Kluger and DeNisi were left with 131 studies. Of those 131 studies, 50 actually documented ways that feedback *lowers* performance, leaving a balance of only 81 studies over nearly a century of inquiry that documented highly effective feedback techniques. As Wiliam (2011) notes in commenting on Kluger and DeNisi's work, this means that "in almost two out of every five carefully conducted studies, the participants would have done better if the feedback had not been given" (p. 114).

The Essence of Feedback

Wiliam (2011) boils all of the research on feedback down to the idea that "feedback must cause thinking" and offers the following three major considerations about feedback:

- Feedback needs to direct attention to what's next, not on how the student did on the work.
- Feedback needs to be focused, specific and clear.
- Feedback needs to relate to the goals shared with the students (e.g., rubrics, etc.).

We use these three criteria to more deeply explore effective feedback. Stop doing what you've been doing with grades and comments at the highest level. One common mistake we often make is pairing feedback, typically comments, alongside projected grades in draft submissions. In doing so, we are being far less than effective. If feedback is best when it focuses on "what's next," why do we feel so compelled to always include a grade that instead focuses on "how well or badly the student did the work?" Wiliam (2011) asserts that this practice of pairing grades and comments, "probably the most prevalent form of feedback to students in the United States," does little to improve performance (p. 122).

Some studies (Butler, 1987, 1988; Wiliam, 2011) document that comment-only feedback, without grades, is among the best overall for promoting learning. When comments are paired with grades, students typically focus on the grade and do not use the comments to improve their work. As Wiliam (2011) notes, "as soon as students get a grade, the learning stops. We may not like it, but the research . . . shows that this is a relatively stable feature of how human minds work" (p. 123).

Cognitive research done by Dr. Amit Sood (2013) at the Mayo Clinic brings another perspective. For survival reasons, our brain "by design, over-estimates a threat's severity and probability and underestimates our ability to respond effectively" (pp. 36–37). The brain likely perceives bad grades as a threat. Grades, then, may create a dynamic where students overestimate the severity of the grade ("I'm a failure . . .") and underestimate their ability to get any better ("I'll always be a failure.").

Brookhart (2008) asserts that in a student's mind "the grade 'trumps' the comment; the student will read the comment that the teacher intended to be descriptive as an explanation of the grade. . . . Descriptive comments have the best chance of being read as descriptive if they are not accompanied

by a grade" (p. 8). Wiliam (2011) explains that, "as soon as students compare themselves with someone else (through grades), their mental energy
becomes focused on protecting their own sense of well-being rather than
learning something new" (p. 128).

So the implication for us is this: "If teachers are providing careful diagnos-
tic comments and then putting a score or grade on the work, they are wasting
their time" (Wiliam, 2011, p. 109). As a culture, though, we are obsessed
with grades. Parents expect them. Course credits are based on them. Although
informed by the research on their negative impacts, many administrators, particularly at the secondary level, still have trouble envisioning a world without
grades. What would a grade-free or grade-reduced world look like?

IMPACT

Consider a world where grades are received less often, or are absent altogeth-
er. Wiliam (2011) succinctly states, "If grades stop learning, students should
be given them as infrequently as possible." He advances that "in elementary
school, the use of grades appears to be entirely unjustified. There are, in fact,
schools that have adopted a grade-free policy in elementary [grades], and
educated the parents regarding the advantages for their students." He asserts
that in middle school "there may be a case for grades once a year" and, given
the course-count and Carnegie-unit dynamics of high school, "there may be
an argument for one per marking period, but certainly no more" (p. 123).

In this brave new world, there would be far fewer grades, but there would
still be continual feedback. Clymer and Wiliam (2007) replaced grades with
a detailed spreadsheet with 10 major concepts for each marking period identified, and red, yellow, and green cells indicating "no evidence of mastery,"
"some evidence of mastery," and "strong evidence of mastery." In the classroom "at any time before the end of the marking period, students can provide
further evidence of their competence" (Wiliam, 2011, p. 125). The full details
are provided in *Embedded Formative Assessment* (Wiliam, 2011), but by replac-
ing grades with another, more effective form of feedback—color-coded spread-
sheets—Clymer and Wiliam (2007) found that students became more engaged
in monitoring their own learning, and achievement went up.

Focused Feedback and Instruction

The next major aspect of feedback is that it should be "focused." Chappuis
(2009) advances, as one of her key strategies of assessment for learning, that
we should "teach students focused revision" (p. 13). We often feel the need

to note every deficiency in students' work, but this overwhelms them and does not align with the way most of the world's experts work to improve. They typically choose to focus on one or two key aspects of performance. Focused revision, then, would do exactly the same thing and focus on one or two key elements of performance.

Chappuis (2009) suggests that we couple "focused revision" with "focused teaching," and this seems to hark back to Lemov et al.'s (2012) practice–scrimmage model. Acknowledge that most learning actually occurs during a drill. Scrimmage to an appropriate degree to determine how students are doing with putting multiple skills together. Use knowledge from the scrimmage performance to plan focused teaching and practice on one or two aspects/skills. Give targeted feedback on those specific aspects of performance. Once you feel that the skills are acquired, begin the process again with another scrimmage and choose new elements of performance on which to focus.

Have a Goal in Mind

This focus in our teaching and feedback is facilitated if we keep in mind another idea from Lemov et al. (2012). Though it seems obvious, they remind educators to "replace [their] purpose with an objective" (p. 42). With the former, the focus is on the activity of the lesson, not the objective. If this is the case, the practice will not be as deliberate.

Under the pressures of planning, teachers can easily slip into an activity focus where they talk of teaching their unit on Macbeth, or the Civil War, or genetics. They plan worthwhile activities to engage students in the learning, but in doing so they also need to keep clear about the specific goals and/or objectives for each daily lesson. Based on observations of exemplary teachers, Lemov et al. (2012) assert that great teachers spend far more time identifying a key objective on which to focus, than on building focused lessons from an objective. They remark that "great teachers understand that you start with the outcome you desire. The strategic decision about what skill to refine is the essence of teaching" (p. 43).

Discussions of "objectives" can seem like a flashback to undergraduate coursework on lesson design and the obligatory writing of unit goals and objectives, but this really is a much higher level discussion. To avoid confusion with granular educational objectives, perhaps *goal* is a better term for what Lemov et al. are discussing. What is your goal for this lesson?

The best lesson goals are described as "clear, focused, measurable, and manageable." When the goal is clear, focused, and measurable, then "at the end of the lesson you can tell, via observation or a quick assessment, whether you have succeeded at teaching it" (Lemov et al., 2012, p. 41). Remembering the importance of giving students feedback so that they can see their progress and be motivated to continue to undertake the rigors of deliberate practice, one can see how much more easily this is accomplished with clear, focused, measurable goals in place for every lesson. If the lesson is a general activity, the feedback, if present, will also be general and thereby not as effective.

Finally, when objectives are "manageable" then the lesson is focused on a discrete, even if small, outcome. Many of the skills and abilities we are trying to develop within our students are complex. Writing ability is a good example. We will not ever teach a child to write in a day, or even a year for that matter. "Only by knocking down all of the pieces of [a complex task] effectively, day by day, will [students] master the larger art" (Lemov et al., 2012, p. 41). In John Wooden's words "You have to apply yourself each day to becoming a little better. By applying yourself to the task of becoming a little better each and every day over a period of time, you will become a lot better" (Wooden & Tobin, 1972).

Feedback Related to Goal

The final essential aspect of feedback is that it "should relate to goals that have been shared with the students," which is also framed as another one of the key strategies of formative assessment: "clarifying, sharing, and understanding learning intentions and criteria for success" (Wiliam, 2011, p. 132).

Chappuis (2009) expands upon this by suggesting that through a variety of strategies we should work to "provide students with a clear and understandable vision of learning targets" and "use examples and models of strong and weak work" to make these targets clear to students (pp. 11–12). As Black and Wiliam suggest, the simple truth is that "low achievement is often the result of students failing to understand what is expected of them" (cited in Leahy et al., 2005, p. 21). Showing a range of work samples that represent various levels of expertise provides a source for students to use and understand more fully.

With merely the repetitions, resistance, and results aspects of deliberate practice in mind, it is clear that planning for and providing feedback on deliberate practice requires significant effort and engineering.

The Case for Formative Assessment

Equipped with new insights on the elements of deliberate practice, it is easy to be overwhelmed by the implications for planning. Coach John Wooden spent as much or more time planning practices as he did running them. This allocation of time represents a luxury not afforded to most U.S. teachers. They typically plan hours of instruction during limited planning periods, in evenings, on weekends, and during the summer. So, where do we focus for the greatest return on our time?

It is nearly impossible to review the literature on effective practice without making immediate connections to high-quality formative classroom assessment strategies. As Lemov et al. (2012) put it, "running an effective practice requires systematic attentiveness to participants' rate of success" because "lack of understanding builds on itself and gets harder to fix the longer you wait" and "requires responding to failure to remediate it as quickly and as positively as you can" (p. 26). Formative assessment creates a continuous feedback loop to both students and teachers and thereby becomes a critical element of master coaching, which we discuss later in greater detail.

> It is nearly impossible to review the literature on effective practice without making immediate connections to high-quality formative classroom assessment strategies.

The Formative Process Works

When considered through the lens of deliberate practice and expert performance, formative assessment is a particularly rich area. The research base documents incredible efficacy. As Popham (2011) notes, "it is clear that the process works, it can produce whopping gains in students' achievement, and it is sufficiently robust so that different teachers can use it in diverse ways, yet still get great results."

Also, years of work have already revealed a body of specific teaching strategies that can operationalize the best elements of formative assessment. Of particular note is the ongoing work of Dylan Wiliam, whose 1998 meta-analysis, coauthored with Paul Black (Black & Wiliam, 1998), was the impetus for much of the current dialogue around formative assessment.

After the publication of the "Inside the Black Box" meta-analysis, much of Wiliam's work has focused on identifying specific formative assessment classroom strategies. His highly practical and accessible *Embedded Formative Assessment* (2011), for example, includes more than 50 strategies clustered in five areas of formative assessment. Rick Stiggins and his colleagues at the Assessment Training Institute (Jan Chappuis in particular) have also greatly contributed to the conversation and bring unique insights on the potential of formative assessment to tap into student motivation (e.g., see J. Chappuis, Stiggins, S. Chappuis, & Arter, 2012). Since 2006, the Council of Chief State

School Officers has been promoting formative assessment work through their Formative Assessment for Students and Teachers (FAST) subgroup of their State Collaboratives on Assessment and Student Standards (SCASS).

While there is now no shortage of guidance on implementing formative assessment, Earl and Timperley (2014) suggest that while many teachers report that they use formative assessment in their classrooms, their practice often does not reflect the best thinking around formative assessment. As practice evolves toward feedback that is clear and actionable, teachers can expect to see students become more conscious of their progress, more understanding of how to move forward, and more motivated to do so.

Reaching

When entering the magical mystery zone of higher productivity, Coyle (2009) observes that folks who are optimally developing skill—who are undertaking deliberate practice—are "engaging in an activity that seems, on the face of it, strange and surprising. They are seeking out the slippery hills. They are purposefully operating at the edges of their ability, so they will screw up. And somehow screwing up is making them better" (p. 18).

When you're engaged in deliberate practice "you use time more efficiently. Your small efforts produce big, lasting results. You have positioned yourself at a place of leverage where you can capture failure and turn it into skill. The trick is choosing a goal just beyond your present abilities to target the struggle. Thrashing blindly doesn't help. Reaching does" (Coyle, 2009, p. 19). What percentage of their days do students really spend in this "place of leverage?" And how can we expand this time?

How does reaching change things so much? In reaching, dynamics are created "where you're forced to slow down, make errors. . . . In such situations, we are clumsy, but the irony is that when we are willing to struggle, slip, fall, and be clumsy, these situations, over time, end up making [us] swift and graceful" (Coyle, 2009, p. 18).

UCLA psychology professor Robert Bjork observes that "we think of effortless performance as desirable, but it's really *a terrible way to learn* [emphasis added]" (Bjork, quoted in Coyle, 2009, p. 19). The notion of an ever-struggling expert in development runs counter to the folklore of innate talent where folks are "naturals." Skill comes easily to the naturals, but only in fiction. The reality of skill acquisition involves much more struggle.

To what extent do we help our students acknowledge how vital struggle is to learning? Do they understand that when they are appropriately struggling, they are at "a place of leverage"? We need to share this with our

> ### PROFESSIONAL LEARNING COMMUNITIES QUESTIONS
>
> - To what extent do we really understand formative assessment as a process and a motivational factor? Have we invested in true formative assessment training?
> - John Wooden observed that "hustle and bustle can distract us from noticing when we're not actually that productive" (Wooden, quoted in Lemov et al., 2012). Based on the ideas of this chapter, how might this be true in some classrooms?
> - Vygotsky (1962/1996) encourages educators to help students focus on "ripening" skills. What insights does this provide?
> - Embracing struggle is a critical aspect of eventual growth and performance. How can we help students be more willing to do so?
> - Subtle shifts in language can result in motivational changes. What's the difference between someone "practicing" for an athletic endeavor and someone "training" for one? What if students "trained for" academic endeavors? Are there activities that create a "training for" mindset related to academics?

students and design some learning experiences that free them of the anxiety of grades, where we can allow them to integrate these experiences of reaching, struggling, and ultimately succeeding.

PROFESSIONAL LEARNING EXERCISE: TURN HUSTLE AND BUSTLE INTO PRECISE PRACTICE

Don't mistake mere activity for deliberate practice. Based on the principles of deliberate practice, according to Ericsson, Krampe, and Tesch-Römer (1993), there are two considerations that must be in place for deliberate practice. Paraphrasing their words, with two simple statements that most educators are quite familiar with in their practice, these two principles of teaching and learning seem almost common sense:

1. Activate prior knowledge to provide a landing platform for the incoming, new information. It will settle easier and earlier with the learner into a familiar pattern.
2. Provide immediate, specific, actionable feedback on results as soon as possible to ensure student investment and continued growth.

Activate Prior Knowledge

In teams, participants create a practice routine for student teachers that illustrate activity with engagement. Have students stand and move around the room, high-fiving others until the music stops. At that point have them turn to a nearby partner. The taller one will explain what active learning is, while standing on one foot and the shorter one listens and gives feedback to the first. Then the shorter student gives an example of an engaged learner, while standing on tiptoes. The taller one gives feedback. This is simply to give variety to the partner activity and energize the learners.

Feedback on Results

Then, these pairings are asked to sit together and find three words to describe *active* and three words to describe *engaged*. Together they write a short piece comparing active learning to engaged learning using their six generated words. Using a pair of pairs, pairs share with the other team, who must respond with feedback. Give some feedback that is immediate, specific, and actionable.

CHAPTER 6

Recovery and Residual

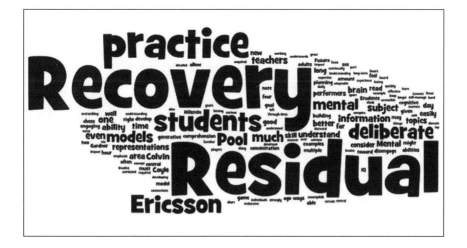

Practice as much as you feel you can accomplish with concentration.

—Nathan Milstein

TIME TO RECOVER

While deliberate practice is clearly a good thing, it is often possible to have too much of a good thing. Because of the constant striving to operate on the edge of one's abilities, deliberate practice, if not properly managed, can easily lead to cognitive and/or physical exhaustion. Coyle (2009) notes that "with conventional practice more is always better," but deliberate practice "doesn't obey the same math" (p. 88).

Deliberate Practice Defies the Math

Ericsson, Krampe, and Tesch-Römer (1993) advise that "to maximize gains from long-term practice, individuals must avoid exhaustion and limit practice

89

to an amount from which they can recover on a daily or weekly basis" (p. 369). Maintaining the intent focus that deliberate practice requires is difficult, and Ericsson and Pool (2016b) note that "expert performers do two things—both seemingly unrelated to motivation—that can help." First, they acknowledge the physiological by getting plenty of sleep and working to keep healthy. Then they "limit the length of [any single] practice session to about an hour" advising that "if you want to practice longer than an hour, go for an hour and take a break" before returning to practice (p. 171).

In the Sweet Spot

Studies across multiple domains show that the total amount of daily deliberate practice time that most people can endure "does not seem to vary," finding that "close to four hours a day" is the maximum (Ericsson & Charness, 1994, p. 741). This applies to most cognitive tasks as well as music and other arts.

> We must keep in mind that spending more time in deliberate practice is only effective "if you're still in the sweet spot at the edge of your abilities, *attentively* [emphasis added] building and honing circuits."

We must keep in mind that spending more time in deliberate practice is only effective "if you're still in the sweet spot at the edge of your abilities, *attentively* [emphasis added] building and honing circuits" (Coyle, 2009, p. 88). Violinist Nathan Milstein advises students to "practice as much as you feel you can accomplish with concentration" (Milstein quoted in Ericsson, Prietula, & Cokely, 2007, pg. 118). Concentration is the key. When you lose your concentration, "you depart the deep-practice zone [and] you might as well quit" (Coyle, 2009, p. 88). Ericsson and Charness (1994) remark that the "master teachers and coaches consider practice while fatigued and unfocused not only wasteful but even harmful to sustained improvements" (p. 741). All teachers have seen students zone out when they reach a saturation point.

NECESSARY RECOVERY

For these reasons, when constructing deliberate practice, Coyle advises teachers to have their students "work in short, intensive, and frequent sessions" noting that scheduling "five minutes each day easily beats a one-hour session each week" (Coyle, personal communication, 2011). Additionally, for most cognitive tasks, the morning is typically a better time for deliberate practice. Folkard and Monk (1985, as cited in Ericsson and Charness, 1994) note that this is "when independent research indicates that individuals have the highest capacity for complex, demanding activity during the day" (p. 741).

It is interesting to consider the control that experts have over their practice schedules as well as the ability to disengage with the activity when they feel it necessary. Students, however, often have little control over their school schedules and disengaging is frowned upon. To the extent that we push students into periods of deliberate practice, we should also consider ways to allow them to self-manage.

THE RESIDUAL AFTER PRACTICE

Finally, let's peer into the darkest, least understood corner of the "black box of expertise development" to explore an element that Colvin (2008) and Ericsson and Pool (2016b) describe as the pinnacle of expertise acquisition. In a far less understood manner than most other elements of deliberate practice, the building of acquired skill after acquired skill, compounded by years of practice, ultimately results in mental models or representations for elite performances. Colvin (2008) notes them as "one of the defining traits of great performers," and Ericsson and Pool (2016b) herald them as "the main purpose of deliberate practice."

Mental Models

Mental models allow chess masters to look at the board of a game in progress and instantly know who is winning, who is losing, and what strategy the losing player could take to possibly win. When observing a chessboard, capable chess players encode massive amounts of information about the game, not through the individual pieces as novices would, but through clusters of pieces that have meaning to them (Colvin, 2008).

Mental models allow baseball and tennis players to read the movements of their opponents and anticipate where a ball, about to be hurled toward them at great speed, will likely be when it is in striking distance and do so before it has even been struck or thrown by their opponents. "A top accountant sees [a particular recent accounting rule change] as part of a broad, post-Enron shift toward more detailed risk management, and understands who it helps, who it hurts, and why it was made" (Colvin, 2008, p. 123). Experts, in short, simultaneously see the whole of the domain as well as its parts, and are able to understand complex relationships.

While K–12 education represents the initial study in many domains and the full development of mental maps will take years, students do begin to experience the beginnings of such connections when they are able to connect major topics or themes within or across classes—they are seeing the big picture.

First the Myelin, Then the Map

"Because the details of mental representations can differ dramatically from field to field, it's hard to offer an overarching definition that is not too vague, but in essence these representations are preexisting patterns of information—facts, images, rules, relationships, and so on—that are held in long-term memory and that can be used to respond quickly and effectively in certain situations" (Ericsson & Pool, 2016b, p. 51). Though hard to succinctly define, the impact of mental models is significant. "A mental model not only enables remarkable recall, it also helps top performers learn and understand new information far better and faster than average performers, since they see it as not an isolated bit of data, but as part of a large and comprehensible picture" (Colvin, 2008, p. 123).

RESIDUAL EFFECTS

Let's consider the impact of models. Make a prediction: How strongly is reading comprehension tied to IQ? Do you think that IQ strongly determines what one is able to read and comprehend? Studies have shown that background knowledge, a basic form of a mental map or representation, actually correlates to comprehension better than IQ (Ericsson & Kintsch, 1995). Your mental model allows you to encode much more information much more easily, even more quickly, than others with a higher reading level.

According to Ericsson and Pool (2016b), "the more you study a subject, the more detailed your mental representations of it become, and the better you get at assimilating new information" (p. 67). Mental models simply grow naturally as we spend prolonged time working within a domain. As educators, we may not have to plan on how to promote the growth of these models, but we must honestly ask ourselves whether we ever dwell on topics long enough for a student to truly begin to develop such models.

> Mental models simply grow naturally as we spend prolonged time working within a domain.

Coverage

Nearly two decades ago, Harvard psychologist Howard Gardner (1999) wrote that we continually battle "that old devil 'coverage'" and that "so long as one is determined to get through the book no matter what, it is virtually guaranteed that students will not advance toward genuine understanding of the subject at hand" (p. 121). He challenged us to create situations where students can "probe with sufficient depth a manageable set of examples so that they come to see how one thinks and acts in the manner of a scientist, a geometer, an artist, an historian . . . even if each student investigates only one art, science, or historical area" (p. 118).

Throughlines

The Harvard Graduate School of Education's "Teaching for Understanding" approach for planning would likely foster mental models. Their framework begins with "generative topics" or those most "worth teaching" (Fusaro, 2008). These topics, or beginning throughlines, targeted at the unit level, should have the following four features:

- Central to a given discipline or subject area
- Connecting readily to what is familiar to students, other subject matters
- Engaging to students and to teachers
- Accessible to students via multiple resources and ways of thinking (Fusaro, 2008)

These generative topics begin the process but mental maps or representations are really fostered through "year-long overarching goals, or 'throughlines'" that teachers continually connect to each unit's topics and objectives (Fusaro, 2008).

Consider the following example:

In an American History course, a year-long understanding goal [throughline] might be, "Students will understand the various considerations and strategies historians use to interpret evidence about the past." This goal can be made explicit to students, helping them organize their thinking, by phrasing the goal as a question: "How do we find out the truth about things that happened a long time ago?" A unit-goal, in this case, might be: "Students will understand how to read and judge the reliability of primary sources about . . ." the American Revolution, or a topic of local history. (Fusaro, 2008)

PROFESSIONAL LEARNING COMMUNITIES QUESTIONS

- If attentiveness is required for effective deliberate practice, what mechanisms do we have for students to self-manage and disengage from practice when it may be warranted? And what concerns are there about this? Could allowing students to easily disengage work against building grit, endurance, and the ability to focus? How do we balance these concerns?

- We all develop mental maps. What examples can you give from your own experience? What mental maps do you help your students construct?

- If the brain seeks to make connections, how are we planning so that learning experiences are connected for our students?

- How has this information challenged you to try and learn something new?

Ultimately, Harvard's planning model is about connections.

When, in life, we have the experience of building concentrated skill and ability in an area, it is very motivating. It's affirming and rewarding to build appreciable skills in an area—to be an expert. Then learning becomes engaging and relevant. But how often are K–12 students afforded such experiences?

PROFESSIONAL LEARNING EXERCISE: THINKING THREADS

Consider the list of the features or throughline guidelines presented above, from Harvard's "Teaching for Understanding" program, which uses generative ideas that thread through the unit, or term. Ask teachers to liken these features to essential questions by developing a T-chart, and listing Generative Ideas on the left, rephrased as a Question, on the right (see Figure 6.1).

Throughline Guidelines

- Central to a given discipline or subject area
- Connecting readily to what is familiar to students, and to other subject matters
- Engaging to students and to teachers
- Accessible to students via multiple resources and ways of thinking (Fusaro, 2008)

Figure 6.1. T-Chart—Throughline Guidelines

Throughlines	Questions
Change is constant	How is change the only constant?
Structure is necessary	How does structure become a necessity?
Pros and cons	Where are the good, the bad, and the ugly?
Everything is connected	What are the connections that matter most?

Part II Classroom Teaching Ideas

What does "practice" look like in the classroom? As teachers, we want to see and read about real examples of how teachers have integrated these critical skills of practice, motivation, and coaching feedback into their classrooms.

Examples at the elementary, middle, and high school levels follow. As teachers and leaders we can support each others' efforts with students by sharing the things we do in our classrooms to motivate and support social, emotional, and physical behaviors that foster the "untapped talent" of every student, and to fully promote student success.

ELEMENTARY SCHOOL LEVEL: MULTIPLICATION FACT MASTERY

Mrs. Kilgore knows that today begins a significant section of learning for her 3rd-graders. They are starting to learn about multiplication. Becoming successful in multiplication facts is essential. Knowing, from her curriculum guidelines, as well as from her previous experience working with struggling middle school students who had not truly mastered basic operations, Mrs. Kilgore wants her students to be multiplication experts, equipped to build new concepts and skills on this foundation.

She knows that there is no magic required, just sufficient practice. Over the next several weeks Mrs. Kilgore has planned a variety of different ways for her students to practice their multiplication facts so she can bring novelty to the repeated practice. Students will use several flash card games, like playing fish and forming relay teams to make it into a contest. They will use the BlueStreak Math software app (Duncan, 2016), with a game-based format that provides instant feedback and then regularly practice with Math Facts in a Flash from Renaissance.

She has also planned a variety of formative assessments to track her students' progress. Some assessments, as mentioned, are instant electronically managed scores, while others are anecdotal observations, data gathering by the students on their own progress, and reflective logs for students to comment on their progress. Nothing should be left to chance about this essential building block.

Mrs. Kilgore has set a high and immovable bar for performance. When it comes to these essential skills, her goal for her students is excellence: Everyone will know all of their facts 1–12, backwards and forwards. The foundation for much of their future success in mathematics is being laid with her next steps.

MIDDLE SCHOOL LEVEL: THE HIGHLIGHT IS HIGHLIGHTERS

Mr. Sanchez's middle school students are focusing intently on the task at hand. The room is silent except for the sound of highlighters squeaking across papers.

Based on previous assignments and on state test data from last year around reading and responding to texts, Mr. Sanchez knows that his students need to do a better job at citing evidence. This is an essential skill with his curriculum and one that will serve students well in life. They tend to find some of the evidence in what they read, but far from all of it.

To help the students focus their attention, Mr. Sanchez has students use highlighters, and he sets the expectation that they will need to read the texts multiple times to answer the open-ended, evidence-based questions he has posed. He has modeled the process of reading the passage once to get the overall idea, then reading the question posed. Students then reread with a highlighter in hand to note evidence or details that address the question before finally writing their response.

If there is more than one question on a text, then the rereading takes on another round with a different color highlighter. Mr. Sanchez firmly believes that the specific process and focused highlighting has made a difference for his students.

HIGH SCHOOL LEVEL: THINKING ABOUT THROUGHLINES

Dr. Gregg's AP Literature students are in the middle of a major research paper. It's nearing the end of the year, and she has used several key themes, or throughlines, to make connections between the various units they have studied all year long. These essential questions have been posted in her room and continually revisited. This project, the culminating piece for the year, is the opportunity to bring together ideas from across the year.

Dr. Gregg knows that the type of work she is demanding in this project is on par with what will be expected as her students transition to advanced university classes. To make sure that her expectations are clear, Dr. Gregg has regularly had the students review and rate sample papers from previous years. She knows that if students can see quality or perceive gaps in the work of others, then that is an excellent indication that her students are ready to undertake their own projects. She did not rush this essential step. When she realized that a significant portion of students were incorrectly rating sample papers, she listened closely to their comments about their review to determine what they were missing—what they did not see. She then planned lessons to help them see these elements.

Well into their own papers, the students have received comments on their work but no final grades. Because of the complexity of the project and what she has seen in their drafts, Dr. Gregg has planned several days of focused revision. Addressing only one element at a time allows her to help her students focus their attention on that element and make substantial improvements in their work. These papers are nearing completion, and Dr. Gregg is very pleased with her students' work.

COACHING:
Seek Extraordinary Excellence

While each part of this book focuses on a specific component of the process of developing expertise—motivation, practice, and coaching—these elements are often, in fact, intertwined and certainly inform each other in practice in real classrooms. Readers may find that the same research sources are cited across the three parts, where the source bears on multiple aspects of expertise development. It is intentional to fully illustrate the intricacies of building experts in any field of endeavor.

Master coaching is integral to the trifecta highlighted in this text. It includes deep, deliberate practice; ongoing, consistent motivation techniques; and the presence and influence of a master coach. While these three are the components studied in elite talents, it seems logical that they also can be applied in a broader, if more modest way, to academic development and growing expertise in students in our classrooms. Master coaching—the component highlighted in Part III—includes three interrelated elements that seem to propel the coaching relationship along a somewhat predictable path that leads the coach and students to engage, elevate, and exceed. First, the teacher/coach and the students engage in a partnership to work hand in hand. Second, the coaching begins to demonstrate results for the students, as the relationship grows and skills are noticeably elevated. Finally, coaches and their students devise challenging reachfulness goals, with methods to help exceed expectations and reach beyond the original goal.

Chapter 7 describes the phase of engaging, when the coach and students become a team, talking and conferring constantly on skill levels, as well as developing deliberate practice routines as a bond of trust develops. The coach and the students must engage in a special relationship, always thinking things through and trusting each other. This dynamic can exist between a teacher and a class, and in other instances in coaching individual exceptional students.

In Chapter 8 the master coach elevates performance with continual and appropriate challenges, coaching, and feedback. To elevate literally, deliberately, and strategically, the coach seeks the best ways to develop and hone the students' current performance achievement through reachfulness, practicing in one's zone of proximal development, at every stage.

Chapter 9 discusses how the master coach moves the students beyond the original goals to exceed the standard or their current skill level. These are the elements at work: goal setting, imagination, metacognitive reflection—all strategies that seem to contribute, over time, to a student's sense of control and sense of agency. The well-known benefits of coaching feedback (Hattie, 2012a; Jackson, 2009) suggest that a master coach–students interaction must be in place to increase the possibility of students fully reaching potential, or enhancing the teaching/learning results.

CHAPTER 7

Engage

Greatness, whether athletic or otherwise, doesn't come from those content on just being, but from those who seek being the difference.

—Kirk Mango

A TRUSTED MENTOR

The student is most likely to engage with the expert teacher/coach she or he connects to personally, to support and develop a specific area of talent or potential. As a trusted mentor, the teacher/coach is there to equip the student with the necessary skills, concepts, and attitudes to succeed, and to ensure that the student progresses along the chosen path. Teaching is complex.

Within this text, teaching and coaching are used somewhat interchangeably, as the discussion targets teachers as coaches in the classroom setting, as well as coaches in the fields of the performing arts. Thus it follows that formative assessment expert Dylan Wiliam (2011) tells teachers, "This job that you are doing is so hard that one lifetime isn't enough to master it" (2011 , pp. 151–152) and Jamey Verrilli of the Relay Graduate School of Education has referred to teaching as "an incredibly intricate, complex and beautiful craft" (Teaching the Teachers, 2016).

The Myth of Talent Folklore

While a recent article in *The Economist* noted that a 2011 survey found that "70% of Americans thought the ability to teach was more the result of innate talent than training" (Teaching the Teachers, 2016), this is one more manifestation of what Green (2015) notes as "the myth of the natural born teacher" and one more manifestation of talent folklore. As with other disciplines, skills associated with great teaching can unquestionably be developed in most people. David Berliner and his colleagues have shown that expertise in teaching shares the same qualities as expertise in other fields (Berliner et al., cited in Wiliam, 2016).

In *Practice Perfect* (Lemov et al., 2012) the discussion turns to the teaching/coaching roles. While in this text the two are somewhat interchangeable and Lemov and his coauthors (2012) believe that both roles—coach and teacher—do contribute to the teaching/learning process, they recommend coaching during the performance as appropriate behavior for the expert, while teaching during the performance as a distraction. This advice has proven to be true. When taking a golf lesson from my brother-in-law Max, the golf pro, he plays the round with his mentee and coaches with comments on what they have already worked on. For example, "Don't forget your footing" or "Keep your grip flexible, yet tight through the entire sweep of the stroke." Then, at the end of the round, he offers a lesson on the driving range. There he shifts into teaching mode and introduces a new piece and instructs during that practice drill. The coaching is helpful in the moment, while the teaching is focused on the range away from the "scrimmage" of the course, taking the learner to a new level.

Similarly, there was an instance when the baseball coach would have his players take the field and execute plays with an imaginary ball. It's a practice technique mentioned in Chapter 4, made famous by basketball coach John Wooden (Wooden & Jamison, 2005) that helps the players focus and pay attention when learning the dull fundamentals of hitting, running, and scoring because they are preoccupied with batting to kill the ball each time they are at bat . . . whether in a practice or in a game.

THE SCIENCE OF TEACHING

Despite the complexities of teaching and the folklore touting the myth of innate teacher qualities, a growing body of research has documented certain skills and abilities that consistently lead to higher student performance. Charlotte Danielson's (1996) landmark work *Enhancing Professional Practice: A Framework for Teaching*, though often adapted as an element within high-stakes educator accountability initiatives, originally was designed to outline "those aspects of a teacher's responsibilities that have been documented through empirical studies and theoretical research as promoting improved student learning" (p. 65).

On the Brink of Greatness

In an intriguing and holistic view about the development of the teaching/learning process, Lemov et al. (2012, p. xv) state, "We are optimistic because we think that the teaching profession is on the brink of greatness." In the writing of this book, we have adopted this incredibly compelling thought that schools are on the brink of greatness, and we believe that the principles revisited in recent publications can, indeed, move schools to greatness. Integrated into classrooms, with understanding, coaching, and fidelity, the impact can be significant.

John Hattie's (2012b) massive collection of over 1,200 meta-analyses (Waack, 2015) has recently attracted much attention to this field of study, particularly with his list of "195 Influences and Effect Sizes Related to Student Achievement" found on Hattie's website (visible-learning.org). Among Hattie's top 10 influences on achievement are formative assessment, effective feedback, and classroom discussion.

It is worth noting that Hattie's ideas are not universally accepted, with some questioning his calculations and others questioning the capacity for meta-analysis to provide detailed guidance (Kamenetz, 2015; Wiliam, 2016). At the same time, Hattie's work provides some general guidance when viewed like an impressionist painting—from some distance, looking for the overall picture, rather than focusing closely and on specific details.

A Winning Way

Wiliam (2016) feels that the best that research can do "is identify which directions are likely to be the most profitable avenue for teachers to explore" and has devoted more than 15 years to identifying high-quality formative classroom assessment strategies. Wiliam (2011) asserts that "the currently available evidence suggests that there is nothing else remotely affordable that is likely to have such a large effect" as focusing on formative assessment. And formative assessment implies getting informative feedback from student work and giving them specific, immediate and actionable feedback for improvement.

Wiliam tackles the complexity of educational research, noting that "in education, just about everything works somewhere, and nothing works everywhere."

The following classroom example illustrates the impact of this high-yield strategy of feedback when used appropriately. Charles was a quiet youngster who seemed to know much more than was readily observable. He seldom spoke up, yet when called on by the teacher his response was always interesting. By giving him some immediate, genuine feedback, "I think your answer is so interesting. Please tell me more about your idea," his teacher found that Charles responded readily during the rest of the class. That's how little things can matter to student success.

Feedback Informs

Understanding the power of the feedback cycle by using formative classroom assessments with her young student, this same teacher began to change the interaction pattern quite substantively. She then thought about trying a formative assessment tool called "signaling" to get feedback from all the students. She directed the students to use finger signals. "Vote with your fingers on these questions. Raise 1 finger if you agree and 2 fingers if you don't agree." With a set of 5 questions, she realized that every student was responding with the hand signals. This was the beginning of frequent use of feedback tools for this teacher.

Any one of the sources mentioned in this chapter hints at key aspects of the science of teaching, but when these quantitative studies overlap one another and also overlap with the qualitative work from the science of expertise, all pointing to common elements, the result is a nexus of the most likely skills required for one to become an effective coach in the classroom. That includes formative assessment tools such as feedback. The strategies all reveal a few areas well worth exploration, in terms of prompting immediate responses from various formative assessment techniques with students. Of course the payoff comes when these proven strategies lead directly to information for the teacher to use in making instructional decisions. This complex feedback loop is the back and forth effect teachers rely on to inform their classroom practice. Moment-to-moment instructional decisions with this kind of instant information from students seem to work well in the dynamics of a busy classroom.

Figure 7.1. Teaching/Coaching Roles

Instruct well, with the end in mind

Encourage improvement with formative assessments

Empower with feedback for responsible action

Inspire with unstoppable passion and belief in the talent

Source: Fogarty & Pete, 2017

COACHING WAYS

Similarly, a sequence that delineates four distinct roles of the teacher/coach, ranges from instructing to encouraging and from encouraging to empowering and from empowering to inspiring the developing talent, as shown in Figure 7.1 (Fogarty & Pete, 2017b). To provide a context for the finesse it takes to become a skillfully effective teacher/coach, a more in-depth discussion of these four roles of the teacher/coach follows.

As teachers and coaches differentiate and personalize to develop expertise in students, they naturally step into the coaching role that is most needed with each student. Teachers usually select from postures to instruct, or to encourage, or to empower, and, of course, to inspire the student, as they tailor their coaching to the situational concerns. This is what an expert teacher/coach does to provide the goal of effective, personalized coaching and feedback for personal growth. These are well-known roles that are intermittently embraced by teachers/coaches in varied circumstances. The four roles are reprised briefly to foster deeper understanding about, and authentic differentiation among, the four.

Instruct—Teach

From verbal input to modeling and demonstration to provide comprehensive instruction about how to perform a skill or understand the nuance in the movement or the math or writing exercise, the expert instructs the newly developing students, as well as high-performing ones. It is the teaching/coaching role that experts assume when they describe, explain, demonstrate, and coach practices with immediate feedback to adjust, reframe, and strengthen a skill. It is how students learn and practice the new behaviors. This is the role that brings to bear all the experience and expertise one has in order to instill the learning in ways that students can implement in their actual performances. This process requires deep knowledge of the skills, as well as authentic know-how to work with this intensity.

"Notice how these are similar and different from what we have been doing."

"Take a look at the requirements and think about your own strength and what areas might be challenging for you."

"Go ahead and try this strategy, and let's see how it goes."

"Don't worry about perfect execution. This is new. We will take it one step at a time."

Encourage—Cheer

Encouragement means many things, but essentially, it focuses on being positive, cheerful, and helpful to the students being served. Kind words, compliments, genuine praise, exclamations, acknowledgments, recognition, and collegial comments are the nourishment that students often need and always want. Knowing that students want to please and that they hunger for supporting feedback is often sensed by the teacher/coach, and it is when the role of encouragement comes in. The cheerleader role is not to be understated or underestimated in its effect, as it is critical to have genuine, specific encouraging feedback for learners working their best.

"Way to go! You seem on top of the day today."

"It's amazing how you handled the complexity of the problem."

"You seem to fit in nicely here."

"Wow, you've already established a good, solid routine."

"I know you can do this. Give it your best and you'll be fine."

At the same time, teachers need to be aware that for every student who is praised in public, many others are listening and feeling neglected or inadequate. Teachers must look for opportunities to authentically praise every student.

Empower—Let Go

Empowering others calls for a highly confident, self-assured leader, because empowering others only happens when one gives away the power to another. The teacher/coach must stand back and allow the student to take the reins, completely trusting that he or she is more than capable of handling the challenge. Empowerment is akin to Vygotsky's (1978) Zone of Proximal Development (ZPD). It is the gradual release of responsibility realized. It's time to let go and believe that the person is ready, willing, and able to pull it off. Much like empowering a teenager to take that first drive out of the driveway, the novice is eager to try it entirely on his or her own.

> "I know how much you have studied this, and I feel sure that this is a great next step for you."
> "I know you have the wherewithal to take this on."
> "I have the utmost confidence in you and am proud of the amazing strides you've made."
> "You have been a pleasure to coach and I feel that this will enhance your personal learning in this area."

Inspire—Whisper

To inspire another is more than happenstance, although sometimes that is how it happens, without even knowing that it did. But an inspired conversation, a gesture of trust and a mention of advancement, a hint of a rareness noticed, these are the remarks or nuanced stories that someone comments on. It could be a teacher, a parent, a peer, a neighbor, an acquaintance, or even a sibling or cousin who sees some unusual talent or skill in someone, and that mere mention could light a spark that may burn forever. It is sometimes an authentic, sincerely stated observation that says it all, and that remark stays with the talent and inadvertently or quite intentionally may shape decisions and forge pathways to a future vision.

> "You have an unusually adept sense of color and tone and texture. I can see you becoming quite the designer if you keep this up."
> "Have you ever thought about a leadership role? Perhaps you might think about getting your certification in lifesaving since you are an avid swimmer."
> "I have never seen such empathy for these others who have had so many disappointments in school. You have what it takes to inspire them, that's for sure."

With these simple examples providing an introductory spectrum of ongoing, on-point assessments that instruct, encourage, empower, and even inspire, it is the perfect transition to a more formal discussion about formative assessment and its major role in developing expertise, talent, and proficiencies in students at all levels and in myriad venues. First, it warrants a look at the research on formative assessment.

FORMATIVE ASSESSMENT

As noted earlier, one area of unquestionable impact in the studies on teaching/coaching concerns high-quality, formative classroom assessment. Paul Black and Dylan Wiliam's (1998) landmark meta-analysis on formative assessment, "Inside the Black Box," documented unprecedented gains when "students [were] taught by teachers who integrated assessment with instruction," resulting in a dynamic where they "could achieve in six or seven months what would otherwise take a year" (Black & Wiliam, p. 21).

Though the term *formative assessment* is not used by noneducators exploring the science of expertise, their descriptions of best practice are replete with references to feedback. In their discussions, they are extremely interested in the power of feedback in motivating subjects to undertake the rigors of deliberate practice. They note that meaningful positive feedback is one of the crucial factors in maintaining motivation and that its presence makes a huge difference in whether a person will be able to maintain the consistent effort necessary to improve through purposeful practice. A simple tale showcases this idea.

When a youngster was discouraged with his self-portrait in art class, he insisted that he did not know how to draw and that he would never be able to make his drawing look like he wanted it to. "It doesn't even look like me," he complained. The frustration was real, yet his likeness was not that bad. Without a bit of fuss, the teacher quietly handed him a brand new set of markers, saying, "these bright colors are all you need to make this an outstanding picture that everyone will recognize as you. In fact, that blue marker is all you need to make those eyes just as sparkling bright blue as yours. Go ahead and see what you can do to finish your portrait."

Encouragement with positive, actionable feedback works when it is authentic and targeted. Similarly, formative assessment authors note how student engagement increases, as does performance, when formative assessment practices are consistently used. Though using different terms and entry points, all of these authors are discussing aspects of the same thing.

Wiliam (2016) asserts that "if we are serious about maximizing outcomes for young people, then the focus . . . needs to be on classroom formative assessment" (p. 63). Stiggins (2014) makes this astonishing claim that is often confirmed by others: He proclaims that "assessment . . . may offer more promise for prompting learner success than any other instructional practice or school improvement innovation we have at our disposal" (p. 4). Clearly, this is an area that warrants deep exploration.

Figure 7.2. Embedded Formative Assessments

Criteria	Clarifying and sharing learning intentions and criteria for success
Feedback	Providing feedback that moves learners forward
Class	Engineering effective classroom discussions, questions, and learning tasks
Self	Activating students as owners of their own learning
Peers	Activating students as instructional resources for one another

Adapted from Wiliam, 2011.

We Have Work to Do

When it comes to fully understanding formative assessment, we have work to do. We have been distracted. As Stiggins notes, "Because that standardized testing light has been so brilliant in our eyes, we haven't seen past it to another application of assessment in schools that promises even greater impact on student learning. This is the classroom level of assessment" (Stiggins, cited in Assessment Training Institute, 2004). We have been so focused on our high-stakes tests and their corresponding accountability that we failed to focus on the classroom level and, according to Stiggins, this is a crisis.

Fortunately, following the publication of "Inside the Black Box" (Black & Wiliam, 1998), Dylan Wiliam embarked on years of ongoing work with teachers to translate the formative assessment research into specific teaching/coaching strategies, just as have many others, most notably Rick Stiggins and his colleagues at the Assessment Training Institute.

Figure 7.2 reviews the five categories of formative assessment through which Wiliam has organized his work.

One of his most recent publications, *Embedded Formative Assessment* (2011), contains 53 specific teaching/coaching strategies clustered in these five areas, as well as numerous additional resources available through the Dylan Wiliam Center (www.dylanwiliamcenter.com).

Basically, Wiliam delineates five fairly common behaviors involving criteria, feedback, class, self, and peers. He believes clarifying criteria for success, providing feedback for student action, engineering class discussions, fostering student ownership, and a culture of peer collaboration among students will set the wheels in motion for assessment for learning in the midst of the normal classroom interactions.

Students as Stakeholders

Very similar in many ways is the work of Rick Stiggins and his colleagues at the Assessment Training Institute, most notably Judi Arter, Jan Chappuis, and Steve Chappuis, While they also focus on translating the research into strategies, they give "student motivation" particular emphasis, noting formative assessment's potential to provide feedback that motivates students.

They feel that this consideration is critical as "powerful roadblocks to learning can arise from the very process of assessing and evaluating . . . depending on how the learner interprets what is happening to him or her" (Stiggins, 2014, p. 17) "Traditional testing practices in the United States . . . cause many students to give up in hopelessness and accept failure rather than driving them enthusiastically toward academic success" (p. 3). Yet, as Fogarty and Kerns (2009) note, "empowering students with understanding and insight about their power to learn and to retain and to apply is . . . true empowerment [that] dictates the skillful and robust use of formative assessments as part and parcel of the teaching/learning equation" (p. xvi).

In seeking to meet key motivational needs, Jan Chappuis (2009) adapted the work of Australian professor Royce Sadler (2002), resulting in three paramount questions that students must always be able to sufficiently answer to maintain and maximize motivation:

1. Where am I now?
2. Where am I going?
3. How can I close the gap?

To illustrate the potential power of formative assessment strategies and processes to answer these questions, Chappuis (2009) then organized the common formative assessment strategies of "assessment for learning" under the headings of the three essential questions as outlined in Figure 7.3. The result is a clear illustration of how motivation is driven through formative assessment practices, "focusing on the student as the most influential decision maker in your classroom" (p. 11).

Where am I? The first question helps students understand the situation of where they are at this point in time, on their writing skills training, their science competencies, their social studies projects, or other learning targets, even as basic as math-fact fluency. Providing exemplars, at this point in time, can be extremely beneficial to students to show them what quality work and below-standard work look like. This could be a set of benchmarked papers

Figure 7.3 Self-Assessing Questions

A Sense of Self-Agency

Ultimate Destination

| *Vision*
Provide clear,
understandable
vision of learning targets. | *Examples*
Use examples and
models of strong
and weak work. |

Current Location

| *Self-Assess / Set Goals*
Teach students to self-
assess and set goals. |

Calculated Adaptation

| *One*
Design lessons to
focus on one learning
target or aspect of
quality at a time. | *Revision*
Teach students to
focus on revision. | *Self-Reflection*
Engage students in
self-reflection and let
them keep track of and
share their learning. |

Source: Modified from chart by Chappuis, Stiggins, Chappuis, & Arter, (2012), pp. 42–46.

demonstrating writing quality, or a simulated demonstration of a science lab experiment, or even a videotaped example of a particular iceskating movement. It doesn't matter what the modeling is, it has a huge impact on the student, just to see the various levels of performance. This is called the "baseline feedback point" for the endeavor whether it's an authentic performance or a student work sample. As always, seeing is believing. That is what tends to clarify and confirm the facts.

Where am I going? The second phase is the time for students to be involved in their own self-appraisal and in the goal setting for their next steps. It is not always recognized as such, but there is no one who should be as keen about setting goals than the student. There is a saying that states that, "If you don't know where you're going, how will you know when you get there?" Goals provide the "goalposts" and they tend to motivate action toward attaining that perceived goal. It's like writing down one's goal. In doing so, the goals are already setting the trend toward succeeding and meeting that goal. It's just human nature that kicks in and moves the learners along so naturally.

How will I close the gap? In turn, students must also continue be involved with available data as they set in place their plans for getting to that final goal. With help from the teacher/coach they can set attainable goals for themselves, always building in that idea of "reachfulness" (Coyle, 2009), placing the goal just beyond their comfort zone, to stimulate that desire to excel as they reach beyond the various steps toward the end goal.

Then the students must strategize about how they can meet that goal and come up with a feedback loop that moves them along incrementally. This is particularly obvious on long-term assignments, such as research papers, science projects, or digital or live presentations. By setting deadlines for various steps, those "phony" deadlines seem real and for some reason they do provide a sense of urgency that gets students moving. In this way, they can see the next step and focus their energies on that with laser-like focus, until they achieve what they set out to do. Performers in the performing arts and in athletics know this process well, yet it applies just as appropriately to activities within the framework of the traditional classroom activities that require developmental growth toward proficiencies and recognized expertise. "We must bring students to a point where they can determine for themselves whether or not they are understanding and decide what to do about it if they are not" (Stiggins, 2004, p. 44). When asked, "What then is a coach, teacher, or mentor to do to encourage success?" Stiggins (2004) replied, "Their job is to do whatever they can to convince the performer that success is within reach if she or he keeps trying" (p. 44). In this manner "teachers must be merchants of hope" (p. 45).

Vice Versa

Why do we try to separate two things that should not be separated? "To be maximally effective . . . instruction must work in continuous, close harmony with good assessment. Optimally, instruction and assessment need to occur almost simultaneously, whereas at present, only instruction is continuous, with assessment attached somewhere at the end" (Stiggins, 2004). In fact, Fogarty and Pete (2017b) use the phrase: "Instruction is assessment" as a pivot-point for a discussion of this idea. While it creates a bit of a conundrum for some, teachers/coaches invariably understand exactly what it means. It means that the two, instruction and assessment, are inextricably linked. They are truly inseparable when learning; progressing and ongoing, step-by-step, continuous development, with appraisal of the steps along the way is the one and only true goal.

Assessment Is Instruction

Think about it more deeply. When teaching or coaching students, their performance provides a wealth of information in the form of "formative assessments" that speak to the expert. By becoming adept at honing the available student feedback, teachers/coaches can zero in on a particular aspect that needs attention and provide the proper coaching feedback to the student that is spot-on. The student knows, then, exactly what to focus on in the next round and moves forward accordingly, or is given more specific, immediate, and actionable feedback from the formative assessing that continually occurs.

SUMMING IT UP

In summary, the ideas of teaching/coaching and formative assessment go hand in hand. The student provides the needed feedback to inform the teacher/coach how and what to react to, appropriately, while the student gets the coaching feedback that gives him or her the next boost for developing expertise and subsequently moving toward his potential talent. It is a continuous loop of the learning, the student informing the teacher/coach and the teacher/coach informing the student about how to best proceed, providing feedback when it's not about a grade (Fogarty & Kerns, 2009).

> #### PROFESSIONAL LEARNING COMMUNITIES DISCUSSION QUESTIONS
>
> - The roles of the teacher and the coach are combined in teacher/coach. Agree or disagree with this choice and justify your opinion.
> - Formative assessment is when the chef tastes the soup. Summative assessment is when the customer tastes the soup. Explain and create your own analogy.
> - Formative assessment embedded in classroom activities, assignments, and, of course, assessments, provides feedback to the teacher/coach to act on. At the same time the student is coached with corrections, adjustments, and modifications that are actionable. It's really a cyclical process. Provide two classroom or coaching examples, one for a whole class where many in the class showed common misunderstandings on a formative assessment, and one for an individual student to promote advancement in a specific area.

PROFESSIONAL LEARNING EXERCISE: INVESTIGATING INFORMATIVE ASSESSMENTS

Use the categories of informative assessments—routine, reflective, and rigorous—and list five examples of student assessments for each category.

Routine—Every day
    Examples: Signaling, Turn and talk
Reflective—Some days
    Examples: Student journals, Stem statements
Rigorous—A few days
    Examples: Test item analysis, Data-driven instructional decision

CHAPTER 8

Elevate

My job is not to be easy on people. My job is to take these great people we have and to push them and make them even better.

—Steve Jobs

GENIUS IN SIMPLICITY

Elevating skill levels and ultimately performance is the inherent purpose of learning and becoming an "educated person." To that end, as we have noted throughout this book, it is urgent to remember at all times that feedback is one of the most powerful tools to elevate student performance. If one doubts the truth of the sentiment "Feedback is the breakfast of champions," think again. At the Olympic games it is rumored that the number of psychologists, psychiatrists, therapists, and coaches providing feedback on every aspect of the performer's state of being, far outnumber the actual athletes themselves. These are the experts in the athlete's entourage that provide constant, professionally tailored, personally customized feedback, adapted specifically for the individual athlete. They monitor the skills, the emotional state, the physical capabilities, as well as the mood, tone, and tenor of their charge, and these people work tirelessly to give them the support that is just right for the circumstances of the moment. They are available, attentive, and on alert at all times to do whatever it takes to elevate the athlete.

Surprisingly, that is exactly how Rick DuFour (DuFour & DuFour, 2012) considered the teachers and students in his care. He believed in a failsafe system of educating youngsters. He saw the teaching/coaching roles as one and set expectations for academic success and well-being for every student who passed through Stevenson High School in Lincolnshire, IL. There are four questions that frame the remarkable work he advocated through the use of professional learning communities for his faculty. The questions he asked were really quite fundamental, yet when first read, they seem ingenious in their simplicity. Paraphrased here from DuFour's original words, are the four questions in our version.

1. What do we want students to know?
2. How will we know when they know it?
3. What will we do when they don't?
4. What will we do when they do?

Of course, embedded in this wisdom are standards, formative assessment, and a call for constant, ongoing feedback for the teaching and coaching needed to differentiate instruction and address the needs of learners.

Why Are Some So Good at What They Do?

The focus of this chapter is on elevating the talent and the competencies of students in ways that teaching/coaching moves them along and ahead toward their greatest potentials, as they progress with the development of their skills, attitudes, and behaviors. Ericsson and Pool (2016b) ask the question, "Why are some people so amazingly good at what they do?" (p. xvii). They attribute the extraordinary skillfulness to "deliberate practice" and use many expert examples and then go on to tell what it means to the rest of us. Their commonsense questions ask: "If you want to climb a mountain, is it best to just take off and find your way to the highest point you seek? Or, perhaps, is it better to use a guide who knows the mountain trails and the fastest, most passable trails for you to reach your goal, and most importantly, who has been to the peak?" One is about lots of discovery and hoping for the best, while the other is deliberate practice with the coaching of an expert. They believe that "anyone who wants to improve at anything, even just a little bit" (p. xxiii) can use the principles of deliberate practice.

Similarly, the focus of this chapter is on expert coaching that targets the various stages of the youngsters' development on their learning curve. We will highlight the fact that the role of pointed, personalized feedback at every opportunity for practice and for honing the skills is essential as the talent unfolds. In fact, this specific, immediate feedback technique requires attention to specific learning progression. With progressions understood, the feedback is improved and enhanced as it targets the progressive path to mastery.

Changes in the Air

Finally, a brief discussion is included to look at future circumstances that call for changes, adjustments, and modifications in the teacher/coach as student expertise ripens. The instruction, encouragement, empowerment, and inspiration must be heightened to keep up with the acknowledged growth spurts and changes. In fact, to this end, there are instances when the actual coach must change to meet the talent or student at his or her level of need at that point in their progression.

VOICES

Researchers, theorists, and writers who have studied coaching and feedback models span a group of highly respected educators noted in this section. Many have spent their professional lives studying and discussing how to optimize student feedback, advocate formative classroom assessments for learning, examine the concept of learning progressions, and perfect teaching and coaching feedback to support and increase student achievement. These leaders include Rick DuFour, Rick Stiggins, Dylan Wiliam, John Hattie, and James Popham.

Yes to PLCs

Professional Learning Communities at Work were developed by DuFour, DuFour, and Eaker (2008). In this collaborative model, they developed a "fail-safe system" for every student. Based on the Deming (1986) model of Theory Z Management, the system must work well if the people in it are to optimize the outcomes. In this case Richard DuFour, former teacher and principal, knew well that school is all about students and student success. "Whatever it takes" became his mantra. As superintendent, he modeled it in every way, as he developed a faculty culture of professional learning communities to support the organizational structures of schooling for, of, and about the students. The follow-up focus on common assessments that evolved helped put the standards in place, and the collegial feedback from the teaching teams unquestionably impacted student success. Over the years, DuFour shaped a National Blue Ribbon High School and had an impact on unknown numbers of schools around the world.

Vote of Confidence

Stiggins's seminal book, *Classroom Assessment for Student Learning: Doing It Right—Using It Well* (2004), was one of the first introductions to formative assessment for many teachers. He believed in fostering and coaching learning, rather than always using summative assessments that are more about grades and rankings. He helped teachers see the value of providing immediate, specific, and relevant feedback for learning. That is what matters most for improving student achievement and giving them that vote of confidence on their best efforts.

Embedded Assessments

In 2015 Wiliam and Leahy released *Embedding Formative Assessment: Practical Techniques for K–12 Classrooms* (in print and e-book versions). Formative assessment plays an important role in increasing teacher quality and student learning when it's viewed as a process rather than a tool. Emphasizing the instructional strategies, this book explores in depth the use of formative assessment and coaching and feedback techniques for the classroom.

Feed Them Feedback

John Hattie's *Visible Learning for Teachers: Maximizing Impact on Learning* (2012b) is a meta-analysis on the impact of multiple "best instructional practices" and their impact on student learning. He delineates and discusses four specific feedback areas, as we noted earlier: Feedback on Self, Feedback on Process, Feedback on Tasks, and Feedback on Self-Regulation. He finds high positive impact for formative assessment, specific feedback techniques, and metacognitive reflections. In his statement about feedback, he calls it the most powerful single moderator that enhances achievement. According to Hattie, feedback identifies specific qualities of student work, guides the students on improvement steps, motivates them to act on the assessment, and develops their ability to monitor, evaluate, and regulate their own work. His words for feedback are similar to many others, yet they have their own nomenclature: constructive, timely, and meaningful feedback. He goes on to say that feedback is valuable when it is received, understood, and acted upon. How students react to the feedback can be as critical as the feedback itself.

Lowdown on Learning

James Popham (2007) wrote an *Educational Leadership* article, "The Low-down on Learning Progressions," that offers much persuasive evidence of their value in formative feedback statements. Popham is best known for his stance against standardized testing and all of the hullabaloo and perceived or real evils that accompany this practice in our schools. He details four phases for teachers for developing progressions: First, identify "must-learn" building blocks that enable the target learning. Second, know that progressions should contain only those subskills that represent the most significant building blocks. Third, trust that the best learning progressions are fashioned according to a less-is-more model. Fourth, to clarify further what a progression is, some refer to learning progressions as progress maps, providing designated stops on the route to the goal.

Such analyses can form the framework for an optimally effective formative assessment process.

Agreement

Leahy et al. (2005) examined the practice of giving timely, relevant, actionable feedback and the effect it had on student learning. The results made quite a stir in the educational world on instruction and have continued the wave toward feedback as an essential element in the learning curve.

IMPACT

The impact of feedback is examined, as well as how formative assessment is geared to potential: From those who claim that they are giving the students a gift with feedback on their performance, to others who talk about how hard it is to give well-crafted feedback that helps, to beginning with limited and carefully chosen feedback as formative assessment.

Friends of Feedback

A literal parade of spokesmen on feedback have contributed to this rich field of finding, of getting and giving feedback, integral to the teaching/coaching feedback cycle. Doug McCurry, of Achievement First Schools, has a trademark phrase that describes what many have experienced in their work as leaders, educators, and teachers: "I'm going to give you a gift, the gift of feedback." Looking at feedback this way can transform the way teachers view it and enable them to see it as a collaborative process. According to Lemov et al. (2012), "Feedback is hard to give, and hard to craft well. But a bit of culture building can go a long way in making it feel like a gift" (pp. 129–130). In fact, it is suggested that one begin in the most expedient and positive way, starting with just two simple stem statements: (1) "One thing I thought was really effective was . . . " and (2) "What if you tried . . . ." In both cases there is no need to couch the feedback for fear of negativity. These statements just lead to confirmation or to an actionable step to try.

Progressive Progressions

Every day, educators make numerous decisions about how to structure learning experiences, hoping to maximize learning. Learning progressions are part of that effort. Progressions seek to outline how learning typically occurs. There is an obvious overlap, but to what extent has the average educator interacted with learning progressions? Popham (2007) remarks, "If you attend just about any education conference these days—whether it centers on curriculum, instruction, or assessment—you'll most likely encounter one or more presenters who tout the virtues of learning progressions" (p. 83). While many experienced teachers develop an understanding of these over time, it is important that we find ways to share workable knowledge of learning progressions with all teachers.

Learning progressions saw a marked increase of interest when the Common Core State Standards Initiative (2010) noted that "the development of [their] standards began with research-based learning progressions detailing what is known today about how students' mathematical knowledge, skill, and understanding develop over time" and that "maintaining these progressions in the implementation of the standards will be important for helping all students learn mathematics at a higher level."

Additionally, Leahy and Wiliam (2011) comment that learning progressions are "helpful, and perhaps essential, for effective formative assessment" (p. 1). And Popham (2007) asserts that they are a "potent way to help teachers plan and monitor their instruction and, as a result, enhance their students' learning" (p. 83).

There's a History

Leahy and Wiliam (2011) suggest that our modern discussions of learning progressions likely trace back to earlier discussions of "learning hierarchies," which Robert Gagné defined as "a set of specified intellectual capabilities having, according to theoretical considerations, an ordered relationship to each other" (Gagné, 1968, quoted in Leahy & Wiliam, 2011).

Modern definitions of learning progressions include the following: *Learning progressions* consist of successively more sophisticated ways of thinking about an idea that follow one another as students learn. In essence, they lay out, in words and examples, what it means to move toward more expert understanding (National Research Council, 2006, p. 3). Also, progressions are described as a series of successively more sophisticated ways of thinking about key disciplinary concepts and practices across multiple grades, which outline "the intermediate steps toward expertise" (Pellegrino, 2011). And finally, the most straightforward description of a progression is that it is the description of how learning typically advances in a subject area (Renaissance Learning, 2013).

Yet, the question remains, can we really document how people learn? Discussions on learning progressions quickly result in some tension between the fact that they attempt to outline steps in learning, while at the same time they acknowledge that there may be multiple paths and some students will blaze individual paths. Leahy and Wiliam (2011) cite an address at the American Psychological Association where then APA president Robert Gagné discussed, and ultimately resolved, this tension in the following way:

> A learning hierarchy, then, in the present state of our knowledge, cannot represent a unique or most efficient route for any given learner. Instead, what it represents is the most probable expectation of greatest positive transfer for an entire sample of learners concerning whom we know nothing more than what specifically relevant skills they start with. (Gagné, 1968, p. 3, quoted in Leahy & Wiliam, 2011)

Quite similarly, Mosher (2011) states that "no one really thinks there is just one developmentally determined 'best' pathway. But many do think that it is possible to identify paths that are particularly productive and more consistent with the ways children and students are likely to attend to and benefit from instruction" (p. 4). This is what progressions seek to illuminate—some of the best possible paths.

Jelly Fish, Tadpole, Sunfish, Dolphin

To illustrate this concept of progressions with a simple example, learning to swim is a familiar process. Remember the progressive classes at the Y? Jelly Fish, Tadpole, Sunfish, Dolphin? Here is a "How to Learn to Swim Progression" that seemed to work best for most of the 4–8-year-old kids in swim classes.

They start with their heads in water, blowing bubbles; then they do the Jelly Fish float, face in water, holding knees tight with arms, just bobbing in water. Then they do the Dead Man's float, belly down, stretched out arms, hugging ears, and just floating like a Tadpole. They then put their feet down and take a breath before stretching out again and repeating the floating, and adding the flutter kick to begin moving forward, and holding their breath until they reach the other side of the pool to become a Sunfish.

The kids repeat these steps many times before adding alternating arm movements at a standstill, and then stretching out to swim with all parts moving, including the arm movements to resemble the Australian Crawl. They repeat this stroke, multiple times, still holding their breath until reaching the other side of the pool. Then they stand again, take a big breath, and repeat to stroke to other side.

When the crawl is done smoothly and with an obvious level of confidence, it's then that the kids learn to rotate their faces in water, then turn for breath as the other arm moves into water; they keep the head rotation small, and the breathing quick. Then while at a standstill they practice slowly bending down to take a stroke, with their head in water, and when ready, they add the flat-out float as they use their legs and arms to swim and take a breath on every other stroke until they reach the other side. They have advanced to Dolphin. Practice, Practice! Practice! Practice each separate skill and do the same slow-motion moves, and then do real time practices with various combinations of movements.

Notice, each progressive step deliberately adds to the previously conquered skills until the entire body is in sync to swim the traditional Australian Crawl with speed, grace, and efficiency. This is a learning progression for a physical athletic skill that offers an observable visual at every progressive step.

Academic Progressions

Cognitive progressions are much more difficult, yet examples are readily available, as seen in Figure 8.1. There are 13 grade levels but 11 standards, as Grades 9–10 and 11–12 are combined (Common Core State Standard for English Language Arts & Literacy in History/Social Studies, Science, and Technical Subjects, Reading Standards for Informational Text K–12, Integration of Knowledge and Ideas - Standard 7). Based on background knowledge and personal/professional experiences, progressions do provide a powerful platform for teaching and coaching.

Figure 8.1. Progressions for Common Core State Standards, English Language
     Arts

_7 Explain how specific images (e.g., a diagram showing how a machine works) contribute to and
clarify a text.

_ 7 Evaluate the advantages and disadvantages of using different mediums (e.g., print or digital text,
video, multimedia) to present a particular topic or idea.

_7 Draw on information from multiple print or digital sources, demonstrating the ability to locate
an answer to a question quickly or to solve a problem efficiently.

_7 Use information gained from illustrations (e.g., maps, photographs) and the words in a text to
demonstrate understanding of the text (e.g., where, when, why, and how key events occur).

_ 7 Analyze various accounts of a subject told in different mediums (e.g., a person's life story in
both print and multimedia), determining which details are emphasized in each account.

_7 Interpret information presented visually, orally, or quantitatively (e.g., in charts, graphs, diagrams,
time lines, animations, or interactive elements on Web pages) and explain how the information
contributes to an understanding of the text in which it appears.

_ 7. Integrate and evaluate multiple sources of information presented in different media or
formats (e.g., visually, quantitatively) as well as in words in order to address a question or
solve a problem.

_ 7 Compare and contrast a text to an audio, video, or multimedia version of the text, analyzing
each medium's portrayal of the subject (e.g., how the delivery of a speech affects the impact
of the words).

_ 7. Use the illustrations and details in a text to describe its key ideas.

_ 7. Integrate information presented in different media or formats (e.g., visually, quantitatively)
as well as in words to develop a coherent understanding of a topic or issue.

_ 7. With prompting and support, describe the relationship between illustrations and the text in
which they appear (e.g., what person, place, thing, or idea in the text an illustration depicts).

Why Progressions?

Perhaps the most compelling case for learning progressions was made when
Heritage (2008) observed that "despite a plethora of standards and curricula,
many teachers are unclear about how learning progresses in specific domains"
(p. 3). The mere presence of standards did not necessarily equip teachers to
understand how students actually learn.

Mosher (2011) remarks, "At one level, the idea of progressions is simple and obvious. Kids learn. They start out by knowing and being able to do little, and over time they know and can do more, lots more. Their thinking becomes more and more sophisticated" (p. 2). Leahy and Wiliam (2011) note that "some learning hierarchies do seem to be inevitable. In mathematics, for example, it seems inconceivable that someone could master multiplication before addition" (p. 7). In other subject areas and with other topics, the most likely progression may not be immediately apparent.

Yet we do know that fundamentals like math-fact fluency do have a natural progression, just as literacy skills tend to move in a progression with vocabulary and fluency preceding comprehension. The ability to identify a problem, gather information, and interpret the findings are protocols, or progressions, that matter in fine-tuning student expertise as productive problem solvers and sound decision makers (Fogarty & Pete, 2017a) in the science lab or the history classroom.

There Is a Learning Curve

It is also known that there is a "learning curve," which suggests that learning is progressive and that learning tends to curve up and then peaks, and then may actually descend, unless used with accuracy and consistency. Of course it seems that that is exactly what progressions are about, that progressive nature of learning as mentioned earlier in the chapter.

Given these dynamics, and looking at content through the lens of progressions, teachers can better "understand the critical elements that underpin academic success" (Stiggins, 2014). As previously noted, "If the teacher has a clear road map that designates pivotal stops along the way, it is far easier to incorporate those stops" when planning instruction (Popham, 2007, para. 4).

Progressions Inform

Popham (2007) points out that knowledge of learning progressions can promote an "optimally effective formative assessment process." Teachers, he asserts, "shouldn't collect [formative assessment] data on a whim. The formative assessment process will be far more successful if teachers *systematically* collect evidence of a student's progress toward mastery of each key building block in a learning progression. If a student is having trouble with building blocks, when based on learning progressions, the assessments can pinpoint why" (p. 83, emphasis in the original).

Mosher (2011) points out how assessments crafted with knowledge of progressions can generate results that are far more useful to teachers and to students. "You would want assessments that identify and discriminate among defined levels on progressions, rather than discriminating among students on general dimensions or traits such as mathematical ability or scientific understanding. . . . You would consider that to be more useful for guiding instruction and giving the student feedback than being able to say 'this student is weaker than many students in mathematical ability,' or even 'this student is at a basic, rather than a proficient level'" (p. 12).

Any Conflicts?

Some may worry that various progressions may not be in alignment with particular standards sets. Leahy and Wiliam (2011) point out that "the level of granularity needed by teachers to effectively use learning hierarchies in their own work is generally at a far finer level than those used in educational objectives." Teachers must decide the topic for each day's lesson, yet, with some standards sets, the lessons necessary to address individual standards often "covered about two weeks of learning for typical students" (p. 7). In fact, in their work with the English National Curriculum, the National Foundation for Educational Research (NFER) sought to take the broad statements of the curriculum and break them down into "several shorter fragments, each of which could form the teaching basis of a lesson plan" (Kirkup et al., 2014, p. 7).

Which One Do I Use?

Given that this is an emerging area of inquiry, progressions vary greatly in form and detail. "There is no single, universally accepted and absolutely correct learning progression underlying any given high-level curricular aim" (Popham, 2007, p. 84), and given various complexities, there likely will never be.

While teachers intuitively feel the need to seek out one definitive learning progression, this may not be necessary. Popham (2007) notes that "almost any carefully conceived learning progression is more likely to benefit students than teachers' off-the-cuff decision making" (p. 83). Simply by beginning to consider things from a progressions point of view and thoughtfully considering the various steps or stages in understanding that students most typically work through, we are afforded new insights on how to best plan our work.

Yet "to be of maximum use to practitioners, learning progressions will have to be developed and validated locally" (Leahy & Wiliam, 2011, p. 7). "What follows is one example of a professional learning, that uses domainspecific nonfiction titles, across grade levels to illustrate how curriculum designers and classroom teachers can infuse the English language arts block with rich, age-appropriate content knowledge and vocabulary in history/social studies, science, and the arts." Extrapolated from college and career readiness standards this example is of one standard, progressing through the grades.

PROFESSIONAL LEARNING COMMUNITIES DISCUSSION QUESTIONS

- "Feedback is the breakfast of champions." What exactly does that mean?
- Each member should write a learning progression for a skill he or she knows well. Discuss the value of that exercise within the PLC.
- Discuss how formative assessments, feedback, and coaching are related for classroom best practices.

PROFESSIONAL LEARNING EXERCISE:
PROGRESSING TOWARD PROGRESSIONS

Using the set of standards that appear on the sheet (shown in Figure 8.1), prepare for the teachers' session by cutting the standards into separate strips. Give each pair an envelope with the strips inside. Ask them to work together and place the strips in order for a learning progression of the standards by grade levels from K to 12. Debrief with a group discussion of how the standards appear in the actual document for Common Core State Standards (CCSS; 2010) and share how various teams were able to determine a logical sequence of progression. Ask for insights about the experience and how it might or might not be appropriate for students to do.

CHAPTER 9

Exceed

The delicate balance of mentoring someone is not creating them in your own image, but giving them the opportunity to create themselves.

—Steven Spielberg (2015)

SURPASSING ALL EXPECTATIONS

This final chapter on master coaching explores the concept of coaching that propels the learner to synthesis, to empowerment, and to exceeding all expectations. This phase of coaching and feedback is consolidated with the deliberate practice routines, continued strategies to ignite and fan the flames of the will, grit to persist throughout the process of developing talent or potential, and the new emphasis on exceeding all limits, smashing records, and giving back. Be aware that this phase may repeat itself again and again, with various contingencies of exceeded limitations and expertise at higher and more sophisticated levels.

It is, inevitably, the phase that may require a change or modification in the coaching relationship as the level of expertise may need further skill extension. It may call for radical change in the coaching team in order to move to a source able to execute the needed coaching expertise for the next exceptional levels of performance. It's almost aligned to moving from a highly skilled coach to an exalted mentorship relationship or the next mentorship. Sometimes there is that rare individual who can continue to shape and tailor instruction, coaching, and feedback for the rare talent. Yet, changing the talent's experts as the development advances is a fairly predictable part of the story of developing extraordinariness.

The Road to Extraordinary

The bittersweet truth is found in the words of K. J. Oldster in "On this Road to Extraordinary": "Mentorships, similar to other important relationships, usually end. Ideological differences and a need to chart a personal path might preclude parties from maintaining the original balance that stabilized a mentoring relationship. Conflict between an apprentice and his master is not always bad; in fact, it is almost inevitable, if the apprentice's destiny is to exceed the accomplishments of the master" (K. J. Oldster, personal communication, 2016).

While these examples of extreme, out-of-the-ordinary talents are few and far between, they do provide glimpses of how these talents grow beyond the highest norms to outlandish levels of performance and typically, at some point outgrow their teachers, coaches, mentors, and most earnest advocates.

Still, as we look toward classroom applications of three tenets or principles of developing expertise, in ordinary classroom settings, teachers, more often than not, do automatically change in the natural progression of students moving along through the grades. Interestingly, it is not unusual to see the potential of some students rocket to new heights with new teaching, coaching, and feedback from this change in teachers.

Full Speed Ahead

The learners have a major role at this point in their journey. They must develop the needed insights to eventually assume ownership of their extreme talent and achievements. They must learn how to develop the necessary humility, pride, integrity, and energy to proceed at full speed ahead.

It is also, possibly, the moment when learners have an epiphany of sorts and truly realize the remarkable talent they have developed. Over many hours of deliberate practice, the motivational instances that continued to ignite the desire to achieve at the highest level and the notion that they have exceeded all boundaries, places them in an esteemed position. It can be quite a badge or, perhaps, burden to embrace. Yet these talented ones have reached a pinnacle in their chosen field, and almost always can and will contribute something new. They set a new high, found a new movement, gift the aspiring talents with new knowledge and creative insights and modest reflections as they ready themselves to "give back" to their life passion in lasting ways. In fact, this phase often becomes the time for their standout performances that take them on a leap into fresh directions of independence, inventiveness, and outstanding gifts to others who may succeed them in the near future.

To exceed with elegance and emerge with ownership of one's learning expertise and remarkable accomplishments, of course, requires a number of essential elements that bring all the practice and study and talent to fruition. Among these are the ability to self-regulate, to integrate metacognitive reflection and other meditative elements into their repertoire of practices, and to develop a strong and enduring sense of confidence and self that builds the concept of self-agency. Each of these aspects of developing potential, real expertise, authentic talent, and the will to do "whatever it takes" to remain at the peak, are the hallmarks of a genuine talent, skillfulness, and expertise.

VOICES

Research and theories from Perkins, Ericsson and Poole, Hattie, and Dweck inform this chapter discussion on coaching and aims to exceed the limits of the skills, know-how, and performance of the learner by providing information and feedback from brain research and cognitive studies to meditation and relaxation components. In addition, there is an examination of several powerful techniques—metacognitive reflection, self-regulation, the development of a growth mindset, and a sense of student agency.

The Big Picture

Perkins (2010), in *Making Learning Whole,* provides an undergirding premise to the concept of exceeding previous skills and performance through coaching and feedback. In brief, it speaks to the need for a comprehensive, big-picture view of the entire sport, musical scene, scope of the study, or of the compelling interest that drives the person to want to excel and exceed the limits in their chosen field. It creates a needed balance with Coyle's (2009) regime of repetitive practice, stroke-by-stroke, piece-by-piece, and Ericsson and Pool's (2016b) work with deliberate practice using coached or carefully engineered routines.

Effects

John Hattie (2012a) reports the astonishing impact that feedback and metacognition have on student achievement. Among the top four are metacognitive reflection, formative assessment, feedback, and cooperative learning.

No Magic Number

Dweck's (2006) contribution around her terms *fixed mindset* and *growth mindset*, fairly well known and evident in many school curriculums across this country and around the world, has definitely had an impact on how teachers try to influence how students look at their learning and their learning potential. With Dweck's work in tow, and among many others who preceded her in the cognitive sciences, we no longer believe in a magical IQ number that one is born with and that was once seen as the number supposedly indicative of one's intelligence. While formerly believed and still assessed and discussed in certain situations, the emerging science on the brain and learning has forced us to set this theory aside for most purposes and to focus on how to change attitudes and build positive self-concepts, self-esteem, and a sense of control and student agency.

Metacognition: Mirror, Mirror on the Wall

Swartz and Perkins (1990), working in the 1980s and 1990s were responsible for studies in the field of cognitive science and, in particular, studies about the concept of metacognition. They revealed an interesting hierarchy suggesting four levels of metacognitive behaviors (see Figure 9.1): (1) *tacit use*, or subconscious use of strategies without really thinking about them, just using them as reflexive behavior; (2) *aware use*, or knowing that one is using a strategy and recognizing that use through metacognition and self-reflection; (3) *strategic use*, consciously and purposely using the strategy to get a desired result; and (4) *reflective use*, thinking back, thinking about what one used before and if the strategy worked or not, and trying to determine if this is the right time to try it again.

Knowing What You Don't Know

While this is a simple hypothesized example, it offers much to ponder about the effectiveness of some performers, students, or learners with their skillful use of metacognition. At the same time, it is just as revealing to observe the absence in others of any real evidence of using metacognitive behavior. The instance offered to illustrate this involves reading by two students, each managing comprehension in their own way (Fogarty, 1994).

> One student reads and reads and reads, and when he gets to the end of the page, he has an awareness, some metacognitive alert system, that

Figure 9.1. The Hierarchy of Metacognitive Behaviors with Examples

Tacit Use: Automatically	Toddlers go into a temper tantrum to get their way and automatically revert to this when they don't get their way.
Aware Use: Know	When the toddler becomes aware of the reaction a certain behavior gets, they begin to sense some form of control over their environment and instantly stops when they are satisfied with the response.
Strategic Use: Premeditated	The toddler maps out a plan to use the tantrum, because they know it works.
Reflective Use: Mindful	The toddler thinks about how they can get what they want and runs through a few ideas: Crying? Whimpering? Smiling? Pouting? Hugging? Begging? And so on until they do what they think will work. If it doesn't, they move on to another strategy.

Source: Fogarty, 1994.

signals him that he has lost contact with the text, and he has no idea what he has just read. With that signal, he employs a recovery strategy, looking for a key word, rereading the first and last sentence or tediously reading the entire page over again, until he is satisfied that he has some sense of the content in the text.

The second student reads, and reads, and reads and turns the page and keeps reading, reading, reading. When he is done, he has no idea that he does not really know what he read. He, literally, has little idea that he is supposed to get meaning from the text, let alone knowing that he is supposed to read in order to get meaning. He doesn't really know that he is supposed to read to understand. He only goes through the motions, but relies on various other ways to learn, including teacher talk, asking a friend, or looking at the pictures and charts to try to discern meaning.

It's important to focus on metacognition and thinking about your own thinking, because the reflective learning that comes with metacognitive behaviors has a very high impact on learning.

16 Candles

Costa and Kallick (2009) in their series on Habits of Mind, delineate 16 "candles" that represent desired dispositions to cultivate in our youngsters, such as posing questions, delaying impulsivity, transferring ideas, persisting at a task. When these habits of mind, which signify attitudes and dispositions, become deeply embedded in the routine behaviors of a person, they actually align beautifully to the principles of this text: (1) Deliberate practice (Aware); (2) Ongoing motivation (Reflection); and (3) Coaching and feedback cycles (Strategic). They are highly positive behaviors to cultivate in our youngsters.

Get It Done

Angela Duckworth (2016) is the "Grit lady" to some. Her concept of invoking the characteristic of "grit" is to foster persistence, perseverance, and stick-to-itiveness with youngsters. The model is about developing the will to "get it done," to keep doing what you're doing, put one foot in front of the other, and don't stop until you reach the end. That's grit from the grind that it takes to exceed as an expert or extraordinary talent.

Down Time

Goldie Hawn (2003), of the Hawn Institute, has collaborated with Judy Willis for 11 years. Both are invested in promoting "brain-friendly strategies in the school setting." These include movement, exercise, downtime, and meditation. Willis and Hawn have presented educational programs together to talk about physical, cognitive, and emotional renewal techniques for students. The focus is balancing energetic work time with the use of downtime, exercise, and meditation, in short, tools to provide balance in the busy, overscheduled school day. In the collaboration, Willis provides the element of her knowledge of the science of the brain and learning and Hawn's Institute provides a program and results on the positive effects of quiet time for the brain through meditative moments integrated into the school day. It follows current thinking on the value of movement and relaxation exercises to rejuvenate the students' energy, attentiveness, and retention.

IMPACT

Geared to developing student potential and growing talented expertise, this section delineates ideas of what the classroom tactics look and sound like; giving real ideas and applications that apply to classrooms—and to the real world. Paralleling the outlined elements in the introduction, this section provides in-depth discussions about self-regulation, metacognition, meditative elements, a strong and enduring sense of confidence and self, and visible evidence of student-agency. Each of these are aspects of developing potential, real expertise, authentic talent, and the will do "whatever it takes" to remain at the peak. They are the hallmarks of genuine talent, skillfulness, and expertise.

Self-Regulation

In reference to one of the most effective teaching techniques, metacognition, Hattie (2012b) seems to prefer to use the word *self-regulation*, rather than the word *metacognition*. He cites the concept of students learning to become their own teachers. "When thinking about thinking, we need to develop an awareness of what we are doing, where we are going, and how we are going there; we need to know what to do when we don't know what to do. Self-regulation or metacognitive skills are one of the ultimate goals of all learning; they are what we often mean by lifelong learning and it is why we want students to become their own teachers" (p.115).

From a practical perspective, having students set goals helps them learn about taking control over their own learning. As part of the goal, they must justify how they plan on reaching that goal and in the process of that step-by-step plan, they become more self-sufficient and on their way to self-regulating their learning. Interestingly, simple routine tasks often have huge effect sizes (Hattie, 2012b, p. 117, excerpt from Table 6.2), as seen in Figure 9.3. To help one interpret these findings, anything approaching an effect size of 1.0 is a strong result.

To clarify, a stanine ("standard nine") score is a way to scale scores on a 9-point scale that spans across the bell curve (Figure 9.2), a traditional graph that shows the normal distribution of a large sample. Typically, it starts on one side very low, swings upward to a high point, and then creates a similar curve downward, to the other side, mirroring the same line.

A full standard deviation or effect size of 1.0 is equivalent to one full stanine of growth on the bell curve. One stanine is considered a year's growth. Any number above a 0.05 stanine indicates a strong effect size. Notice the

Figure 9.2. Bell Curve with Stanines

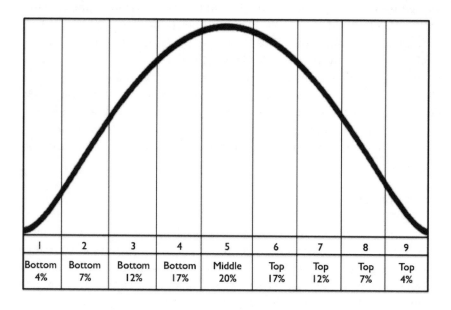

1	2	3	4	5	6	7	8	9
Bottom 4%	Bottom 7%	Bottom 12%	Bottom 17%	Middle 20%	Top 17%	Top 12%	Top 7%	Top 4%

bell curve with stanines marked (see Figure 9.2) and the chart about how to interpret the stanine scores (see Figure 9.3), and, finally, Hattie's chart, indicating the power of metacognition to impact learning (see Figure 9.4).

Metacognitive Reflection

As we think about metacognition, try to remember the first time you heard the word. Where were you? What was the context? How would you explain it to someone who had never heard the word? What exactly is *metacognition?*

The first thing we hear, and probably repeat, as mentioned earlier, is "metacognition is thinking about your thinking," or we might say, "Metacognition is learning about how you learn." Some prefer to say it is about being aware of the "whys" and "hows" of the "what." To clarify with an example, it is being aware of the task of writing an essay, but also being aware of how slowly you are going and wondering why you chose that particular topic that you knew so little about. It's that stepping back, or stepping aside, and reflecting on what you are doing. And it's difficult to exercise cognitive skill

Figure 9.3. Stanines Conversion

Step 1: Rank the scores from lowest to highest.

Step 2: Assign a stanine score to your scores from:

Percentage	Stanines	Rating
Top 4%	9	
Next top 7%	8	High
Next top 12%	7	
Next top 17%	6	
Middle 20%	5	Average
Next bottom 17%	4	
Next bottom 12%	3	
Next bottom 7%	2	Low
Bottom 4%	1	

Note: The mean lies in the middle of the fifth stanine, cutting the center 20% into two parts.

Figure 9.4. Metacognition: Effect Sizes and Strategies

Classroom Behaviors	Effect Sizes	Strategy
Making an Outline (Planning)	.85	Sequence Ideas
Delaying Gratification (Work First)	.70	Write Down Reward
Self-Verbalizing (Saying Steps)	.62	AB Serve and Volley
Self-Evaluation (Checking Work)	.62	Peer Editing
Help-seeking (Study Partner)	.60	AB Alternating Partner
Keeping Records (Note-taking)	.59	Student Excel Data Sheet
Rehearsing Memorizing (Memory Cues)	.57	Memory Pegs

Source: Lavery (2006), in Hattie (2012), p. 116.

and metacognitive reflection at the same time. Yet making students acutely aware of the need to plan what they are going to do, and to monitor themselves as they are doing it, and then to reflect and evaluate how it went, is part and parcel of becoming a self-directed, competent, or even proficient learner. Figure 9.4 presents the metacognitive data that is extrapolated from Hattie's table with our addition of clarification words (in parentheses) and specifically named strategies.

Thinking About Your Thinking

Learning to become metacognitively aware of one's actions, thoughts, words, and deeds, as well as one's behaviors, habits, attitudes, and aptitudes, depends on the effectiveness of an individual's power of insight into himself or herself. It also depends on one's integrity to be entirely candid about what is obvious, and the ability to find the inspiration to proceed. This takes a healthy, mentally aware, and highly motivated person. It takes effort and effectiveness to hone this set of skills. It is about becoming a self-realized learner. It is a process that teachers can help students develop with reflective strategies and grow an *awareness* of self and the *control* measures to take when change is indicated.

The set of stem statements or reflective questions in Figure 9.5 prompts students and students working in small groups to think about their learning: what went well and what might need a change, and so on. These metacognitive skills are embedded in the strategies that students learn to use. This listing is partial, but these are appropriate for K–12 students and adults to get them in the reflective mindset for self-awareness, self-improvement, and self-appraisal. Of course all skillfulness in knowing oneself leads to more powerful learning and a true sense of student agency.

It's About Me

One of the behaviors to help students exceed their limitations and their goals, is to personalize the performance in some way that becomes their brand. This personal mark evolves when the learners are quite advanced in the basic fundamentals of their craft, sport, academic subject, or whatever their designated area of expertise. In establishing a personal brand or symbol—a recognizable, identifiable "trademark"—the level of confidence, self-esteem, and sense of self surfaces and often provides that extra boost to strive for even greater advancements. When this progress is incremental, as it usually is at these levels of performance, the positive impact of personalization cannot be underrated. It identifies this person as singularly extraordinary in his or her field of endeavor.

Figure 9.5. Reflection Strategies

Mr. Parnes's Questions: How does this connect? How will you use it?

Mrs. Potter's Questions: What's the goal? What went well? What will change next time?

Ms. Poindexter's Questions: When did you get stuck? How did you get unstuck?

What? So What? Now What? What Data? So What? Infer: Now What? Act.

Aha! Oh, No! Aha! What was striking? Oh no! What are the implications?

PMI: Plus? Minus? Interesting?

3-2-1: 3 Recalls, 2 Questions, 1 Take Away

Dial 4-1-1 Information: 4 Agreements, 1 Disagreement, 1 Application

Yellow Brick Road: Under Construction, Rocky Road, Yellow Brick Road, Highway to Heaven

Tiny Transfer Book: Take Away 1, 2, 3, 4, 5, 6

Give One, Take One: Partners Give 1 Idea, Take 1 Idea

That's a Good Idea: "That's a good idea because . . . ."

One-Minute Write: Write for one minute, count words, repeat and compare data

---

Source: Bellanca, Fogarty, & Pete (2012).

Strong and enduring self-identifiers may vary from something as simple as one's written signature (often a middle school exercise that teens practice relentlessly) to a "signature" saying or way of shooting the basketball, or even to all the tiny tweaks we make as human beings to stand out from the crowd: what we wear, how we comb our hair, or even favorite colors that become our coat of armor. In our support of developing expertise in students, teachers must encourage this kind of individuality to foster the growth of confidence in their overall talent, their outstanding skills, and their ongoing growth into who they are and who they will become.

I Fail, I Recover

Building and fostering the idea that "I can fail and recover, I can stick to it and figure it out, I can keep going, I'm almost there," are the signs of a growth mindset (Dweck, 2016) that understands the abilities of the human being to excel, to elevate, and to exceed. Students with fixed mindsets that harbor negative impressions of themselves must be supported in ways that help these youngsters see, accept, and celebrate their achievements and their worthiness. Be forewarned, this is often a painstakingly slow recovery for students who feel bad about themselves. Yet it is absolutely critical to their growth toward excellence. Compliment, encourage, flag signs of progress, and be extremely observant and vocal about all of the things the student does or produces that provide evidence of positive movement forward. Small successes mount up and turn student feelings into thoughts about succeeding and how success is possible. Minds change; they change as the dendrites grow and interconnect. Growth mindsets can be nurtured by consistent and persistent positive feedback.

Self-Agency

Also known as the "phenomenal will," self-agency is the sense that some actions are self-generated. Scientist Benjamin Libet (1985) was the first to study self-agency. He discovered that brain activity predicts action before one even has conscious awareness of his or her intention to act. In other words, *self-agency* is an awareness of the acting self.

In fact, a sense of agency or control is defined as "the sense of oneself as the agent of one's own actions." This also allows one to feel distinct from others and contributes to an optimization of self-esteem. This is aligned to the idea of students becoming independent actors in their roles in all aspects of life. This includes behaviors that teachers and coaches must develop to truly support students achieving a sense of self-agency. This means they must learn the art of stepping back, not rescuing; providing space for the individuals to literally "figure it out"; showing faith in the students' decisions, not second-guessing; and genuinely "letting go" and letting the students problem-solve and decide on their own. Self-agency involves student actions that are self-initiated, self-directed, self-monitored, and self-evaluated. While it may include such intelligent behaviors as seeking advice or looking at exemplars or even taking tests, the overwhelming evidence points to a gradual movement toward self-agency.

Giving Back

A frequent occurrence of a talent exceeding the norm or even of a student in the classroom exceeding the standard is the idea of giving back. These high achievers many times expand the field with an extraordinary performance that has some remarkable and new element that will soon become an expectation for others that follow. An outstanding student may develop a memory strategy or some innovative method for learning to share with others. When this is encouraged by the teacher/coach, it is not seen as showing off or bragging; rather, it is seen as a valuable key to help others.

Newcomers do and will continue to aspire to achieve the same accomplishment that they have seen. It will at some point become part of the expectation for excellence, and, in fact, the best of the best will know that this is the new bar that has been set. This is the generative process that talents give back to the field in lasting ways. Twenty-first-century breakthroughs in digital-rich tools that are now available provide visual proof for data-driven feedback to inform their deep practice or to ignite new levels of drive and grit, and, of course, to enhance master coaching that supports the talent to create the newest and highest level of performance.

PROFESSIONAL LEARNING COMMUNITIES DISCUSSION QUESTIONS

- How might we infuse reflection and metacognitive awareness into every lesson? How do we make the time to include this as an integral part of daily learning, remembering that reflective time is when consolidation begins to occur in long-term memory?
- Are we ready for students to exceed? Do we know what to do with them to keep them "in the game" and not be bored to tears? Discuss the strategies you use to challenge these students who are already ahead of the game.
- On a scale of 1–10, how much do you know and understand about what to do to foster student agency? What are some things the team can do to fully embrace this emerging concept of student agency? Why do we want to support student agency?

PROFESSIONAL LEARNING EXERCISE: MAKE A STATEMENT

Adapted from a chart by Sylvia Duckworth (2016), this list can be shared within the teacher teams and subsequently with the students as we try to move the classroom culture from a fixed mindset to a growth mindset (Dweck, 2006):

1. What am I missing?
2. I'm on the right track.
3. If not me, then who?
4. I'll use some of the strategies we've learned.
5. This may take some time and effort.
6. I know I can do this.

7. If ___can do this, I can.
8. I can always improve, so I'll keep trying.
9. I'm going to train my brain in math.
10. Is this a "personal best"?
11. I'm going to figure out how she does it.
12. How can I speed this up to make the deadline?
13. Am I improving all the time?
14. I'm getting better and better at this.
15. What a great result. Wow!
16. Is it really my best?
17. Failure is how I learn.
18. I'm OK, you're OK.
19. Mistakes help me learn better.

Part III Classroom Teaching Ideas

What does coaching look like in the classroom? To fully embrace the concept of coaching youngsters to unlock talent is to demonstrate ways to support it in the classroom. As teachers, we want to see and read about real examples of how teachers have integrated these critical skills of practice, motivation, and coaching feedback into their classroom. With that in mind, below are examples at the elementary, middle, and high school levels for readers to peruse, discuss, and try.

ELEMENTARY SCHOOL LEVEL: THE COACH'S CHART

Introduce The Coach's Chart as a way to engage with a well-known concept: friendship. As you read The Coach's Chart, asks students to *signal* their response by holding up the green card if it's a GO, or yes, they agree, or by holding up the red card if it's a STOP, or no, they don't agree. By scanning the room during the student signals, the teacher/coach gets a *quick read* on where the students are in their understanding and thoughts about friendship. It is also feedback to optimize the teacher's next step.

1. Good friends get mad at each other. Agree/Disagree. Tell me more.
2. My friends are different from me. Agree/Disagree. Explain.
3. My favorite stories are about friends. Agree/Disagree. Why or why not?
4. My brothers and sisters are my friends, too. Agree/Disagree. Describe.
5. The opposite of a friend is an enemy. Agree/Disagree. Give an example.

This provides feedback for the teacher to share ideas, reflections, and key points with the group. Students perform with the signaling cards, then, as the coach, the teacher assesses the responses and infers what is implied. From there, make your "coaching remarks" that seem pertinent to the students.

After the first chart, take this exercise to a higher level and create a similar Coach's Chart to illuminate aspects of a science or social studies unit. Use more content and thinking processes as the kids learn how to evaluate, have an opinion, and support their response with facts or more details.

MIDDLE SCHOOL LEVEL:
VOTING FOR EDUCATION

Use this easy, digital-rich tool to coach and elevate student use of the electronic voting they so often use for entertainment on television shows. The teachers/coaches gain insight from the feedback they get as students respond electronically and then discuss answers orally. It becomes a feedback tool for the teacher/coach to respond with clarifications, to remind students of key concepts, or to demonstrate the execution of the skill. It's a typical teacher/coach situation once the teaching has occurred. The students perform on Edu-Poll for the coach's correcting or tweaking remarks. It offers a viable model of using technology and digital tools for educational tasks in contrast to the multitude of entertainment tasks students use daily.

Create a free Edu-Poll account on www.pollev.com and write your first poll. You can ask an opened-ended question and provide multiple-choice answers for students to text a response on their computers or tablets to respond to the query. Class discussion or small-group discussion follows as the data appears on the screen or is displayed after all votes are in. Then the coach closes the debriefing with critical insights to ensure understanding.

> Sample: The three branches of the U.S. government provide checks and balances on each other, but I think _____ is the most important branch. Be ready to tell why.
> 1. Executive Branch
> 2. Legislative Branch
> 3. Judicial Branch
> 4. President Branch
> 5. Congress Branch
> 6. Supreme Court Branch

After a robust discussion with students about the responses they chose or the reasons for the responses they gave, the teacher/coach can tell a lot about their level of knowledge and understanding by the choices they made and the reasons they gave. Did they choose the proper names of the branches of government or the generic names. Proper names evidence higher levels of academic vocabulary, while by using the more descriptive names of the branches, students may be showing a deeper understanding of what the branches do. Only the expert coach can provide the finely tuned feedback for these students, with the coaching of final details, information, or corrected ideas for the class.

HIGH SCHOOL LEVEL: ONE-ON-ONE COACHING

One-on-One Coaching Unit Review

Use a one-on-one activity as a formative assessment tool for a quick class review of a unit just before a test the next day. The oral exchange of ideas about the content as students respond to questions posed provides two points of view for each learner. Write One-on-One Coaching Questions for a social studies, science, math. ELA, or tech unit for students to execute in the classroom by moving from one student to the next for response; have each student initial the papers of each partner as they move around the room.

One-on-One Coaching—Technology

Find a coach, someone who . . .

1. has a new awesome app they are using in a specific class and evaluate it.
2. knows how to use Easybib for their report and shows it on the screen.
3. is able to develop their report slides into a movie on Animoto and explain.
4. compares and contrasts Snapchat, Instagram, and Facebook.
5. has translation access to another language and will use it to show you.
6. designates favorite fonts for various tasks and justifies each choice.
7. compiles a list of 3–5 apps appropriate for a class and shares it in professional learning community.
8. uses Siri effectively for a number of tasks and will show you how.

Closing

As Yogi Berra is said to have remarked, "It's difficult to make predictions, especially about the future." That said, by examining the session list of any recent education conference, one will easily see the growing interest in personalized learning and the seamless integration of technology into digital-rich classroom lessons, projects, assignments, and assessments of all kinds, and particularly in real-world explorations, investigations, and innovations. Numerous challenges exist, however, for both these emergent interests: (1) personalization of learning for future citizens and (2) seamless integration of technology for a digital-rich world.

Personalization

First of all, we hear of both "personalization" and "individualization." Are these synonymous or are there differences? How does this all relate to previous efforts around "differentiation"? In attempting to bring some degree of clarity, we advance that *differentiated learning* is a broader term that may or may not involve either *personalization* or *individualization*, terms that we will treat as more intensive forms of *differentiation*. Then there is the question of research in this area. Hattie (2012b) claims "the evidence supporting individualized instruction . . . is not so supportive" and overall he calculates an effect size (d) of 0.23, below his "rule of thumb" effect size of 0.4 for the programs of most interest. Yet the studies Hattie (2012b) cites within his narrative, with publication dates ranging from 1977–1986, may not be that relevant within the discussions. The current interest in furthering individualization and personalization is inseparably linked to technology as the tool to facilitate this, so the older studies cited by Hattie may no longer align to the current availability of technology enrichment.

One of the freshest and most compelling cases for personalization is found in Todd Rose's (2015) amazing story, reported earlier, of the U.S. Air Force's attempt to build a cockpit for the "average" airman.

145

Lieutenant Gilbert S. Daniels, because of his background in science, was charged with taking the measurements of over 4,000 airmen on 10 different dimensions (e.g., height, weight, thigh circumference). He then analyzed the data to determine the dimensions of the "average" pilot "generously [defining average] as someone whose measurements were within the middle 30 percent of the range of values for each dimension" (Rose, 2015, p. 4). The approach was very logical. The final outcome defied logic.

Daniels himself was not convinced that the methodology, which clearly emphasized averages, was sound, yet most of his fellow scientists "expected that a sizeable number of pilots would be within the average range on all ten dimensions" (Rose, 2015, p. 4). As a final analysis, Daniels then compared each individual airman's measurements to the average and was shocked to find that out of 4,063 airmen, not one of them was "average" on all ten dimensions. When the threshold was lowered to being average on 3 dimensions, less than 3.5% of pilots were deemed average. Daniels ultimately proved "there was no such thing as an average pilot" and "if you've designed a cockpit to fit the average pilot, you've actually designed it to fit no one" (Rose, 2015, p. 4).

Through this and other examples, Rose (2015) challenges long-held views about averages, proving that complex traits, like intelligence, can never be captured by a single metric. He then illustrates how we are all far more complex and varied than we may ever have realized, with many of our traits changing depending on context. If the Air Force cannot use averages to build a cockpit that will fit its pilots' physical attributes, how likely is it that a standardized program within a school will meet students' varied cognitive needs?

Rose (2015) then provides a fascinating history of public education, highlighting in unique ways the emergence of the factory model and its impacts, both positive and negative. He notes that the factory model "established a classroom environment that made Americans out of millions of immigrants and raised the number of Americans with a high school diploma from 6 percent to 81 percent" (p. 57). He ultimately asserts, however, that we have tweaked and improved on the factory model past its usefulness. The old model is based on "averagarianism." He advances a new age, "The Age of the Individual." In schools, that will mean a transition from the factory model to one that is far more personalized.

That takes us to a brief look at the impact of technology as a personalization tool. In this world of anytime, anyplace learning, there are two arenas to discuss: One is the role of teachers in this era of digital takeover in the classroom, and the second is a quick glimpse at some of the tools, techniques, and troubleshooting.

The Case for Technology

Historically, coaches or teachers would observe and then relay information; they would provide feedback gathered from visual observation of an athlete's or student's skill, relying solely on their ability to perceive changes in performance and interpret the results.

Integrating new ideas and techniques, especially innovations in technology, is a characteristic of an expert coach. Video capabilities make it possible for a coach to record student performance and then play it back for them immediately, while the coach directs them to the key points being addressed in a particular deliberate practice session. Computer-based systems integrate quantitative performance data with video images. These systems can be tailored for use with any sport or task using performance indicators of interest to the coaches and learners.

In sports, these innovations have shaped the way data is collected and processed, how information is relayed between coaches and staff or to athletes, and has had a big impact on the way in which athletes are monitored in the daily training and competition environments (Giblin, Tor, & Paddington, 2016).

The timing of providing feedback is a key concept within motor learning including athletics, dance, and playing musical instruments. Feedback can be classified according to the time point of its provision, with concurrent feedback being provided during skill execution, while terminal feedback is provided after skill execution (Magill & Anderson, 2017). One of the major trends in sports technology has been centered on real-time applications and devices that have the ability to provide athletes, coaches, or scientists access to immediate data.

Video of a deliberate practice session and its analysis by the coach has the benefit of providing feedback flexibly, either during the session, afterwards as a reflection, or as a tool the student can refer to when practicing on this own. Feedback from the coach using the video evidence given as soon as the practice has ended or during the actual session accelerates the authentic application of the particular goals of the practice session. To develop expert immediate feedback is essential for the coach and the student, and nothing provides relevant feedback like video evidence.

Video feedback can also be used in competition to improve performance. Video technology developed prior to the London Olympics in 2012 uses a series of machine vision video cameras and force plates to record the motion of a diver. High-speed video feedback of the dive is available to the coach and athlete immediately after the dive, allowing both slow-motion review and dive comparisons to be made (Giblin, Tor, & Paddington, 2016).

Players and coaches have taken full advantage of the innovations in video playback technology to the point that their practice is on another level.

Sensors engineered into the clothing of an athlete enable measurement of speed and movement in real time. These data can then be exported to develop customized feedback that in some cases includes actual animations of the error that was made juxtaposed beside the correct form.

Studies on the effectiveness of video-supported coaching are in their infancy, but one study was designed to examine the efficacy of video instruction relative to that of verbal and self-guided instruction. Before training, 30 golfers were assigned at random to one of three groups: video, verbal, or self-guided instruction. *Video instruction* was defined as a practice session in which the teacher was aided by the use of video. *Verbal instruction* was defined as practicing with the teacher providing verbal feedback. *Self-guided instruction* was defined as practicing without the aid of a teacher. The participants had a pretest, four 90-minute practice sessions, an immediate posttest, and a 2-week delayed posttest. The results showed that all groups were equal on the pretest. On the second posttest, the two instruction groups performed better than the self-guided group, with the video group performing best.

Troubleshooting Technology

Digital learning brings with it the task of troubleshooting the many ramifications that accompany initiatives and innovations in the school settings. Teachers already sense a major impact on that traditional classroom approach of the previously prevalent, didactic teaching style. The technology tsunami sets the context of the future and for the implications of teaching for greatness as the new paradigm emerges.

A profile in Edutopia in a post (Palmer, 2015) about the modern-day educator, suggests habits of mind that teachers might want to develop in order to survive and hopefully thrive in this 21st-century surge that continues to pick up momentum. Here is the portrait of the modern-day teacher, now, and perhaps in a future vision.

"21st century teachers are not experts in technology, they are experts in habits of mind" (Anderson, 2016). Yet in a rapidly changing educational landscape, modern educators should do the following:

1. Choose to be vulnerable
2. See themselves as colearners not teachers
3. Allow themselves to fail, often
4. Not wait until they're experts to introduce something

5. Move into their students' world even if it's foreign territory
6. Run toward their area of weakness not away from it
7. Be comfortable not knowing what is going to happen
8. Invite mistakes into their lives
9. Dream big and ask, "Why not?"
10. Allow their students to teach each other
11. Step outside their comfort zone
12. Embrace change
13. Feel secure asking their colleagues for help
14. Model resiliency and perseverance
15. Question everything
16. Believe they can learn anything, given the right attitude and effort

This listing offers the opportunity to reflect on the changes for teachers and how these align to the tenets of teaching for greatness and developing student expertise. What is the connection of each of these dispositions with the future vision of modern teachers? This is an explanation of the transition from the sage on the stage to the guide on the side, to coach in the field, modeling a learning individual in the learning organization. How does this jibe with the teacher/coach relationship discussed throughout the book? How does it link to the idea of structuring deliberate practice, continually igniting student motivation, and providing personal coaching for excellence?

The answer is, it does jibe and, at the same time, it doesn't jibe. It does link, and it doesn't link. Sage on the stage, No! Guide on the side, Yes! but *alongside* is more accurate for the modern teacher. And, in terms of aligning with the personal coaching element of developing excellence, it definitely does do that, with the openness reflected for the modern-day teacher, specifically, for the rapidly changing landscape with the student or talent.

Even more remarkable is the modern teacher embracing the posture of a learning individual in a learning organization. We see evidence of that today with the wave of professional learning communities influencing teacher collaborations and many other behaviors in that listing: the willingness to fail and to try, to ask, to be uncomfortable, to question, to dream, to believe, and to embrace resilience and perseverance. These are all labeled marks of future-oriented thinkers and leaders, and all are true signs of contemporary approaches to teaching, lingering in the wings of the teachers' rooms and the PLC gatherings, predictably soon to be center stage.

The teaching and learning scene must change. It is trying to change. It will continue to change, and this ever-present phenomenon called change is truly the only constant in this formula of the future.

FUTURE VISION

Engaged student learning has an evolving new look, too. According to Aleta Margolis (2015) in *The Washington Post*, this is what an excellent classroom engaged in real learning looks like: independent problem solving, students struggling and persevering, physical movement and serious play, students imagining creative approaches to challenges, real-world connections, a wide variety of student work and types of assessments, student-led discussions, and social–emotional skills and empathy.

Again, we must ask the logical question about whether or not these rich examples of student engagement do or do not compare to the principles of the talent code: deliberate practice, ignition, and master coaching of the engaged learner. And, again, the answer seems to be they do, and they don't. It depends, like so many other complexities of the teaching–learning equation. Yes, these examples evidence engagement and do parallel the robust discussion in some ways. In particular, "students struggling and persevering" is much like the multiple discussion of repeated iterations; the concept of perseverance is embedded in the concept of "reachfulness." Reachfulness calls for the learners to push forward just beyond the comfort zone, each and every time they practice.

In another instance of the alignment to the principles of the talent code, students using creativity to address challenges often results from the interaction between the coach and the learner, while in the next comparison, the physical movement and serious play seem to describe the scrimmage and the deliberate practice session, providing the whole-to-part, part-to-whole model of learning within a meaningful context. In a final match from the student engagement model of student-led discussions and social–emotional skills, the three last chapters seem to wrap around with the need to socially engage with coaches and teachers, as well as demonstrating empathy and genuine admiration of peers as discussed when "elevating skills." Through aspirations, talented youngsters yearn to be "as good as" or "even better than" a peer, and at the same time they must internalize the feeling of true empathy when peers are struggling, injured, or hurting in some visible way.

In a summation of these enlightening ideas about the future outlook for teachers and for students, in our view, we seem to be finding the right pathways to encourage, foster, and, when necessary, advocate for these future visions of accomplished, joyful, entrepreneur-bound youngsters who will serve the country well with their creative gumption, critical eye, and persevering ways.

As this chapter comes to an end, it is our hope that this text provides readers with a sense of urgency in obtaining the real goals of the overarching message. Our unfettered goals are to ignite the desire for student greatness;

provide the deep, deliberate practice for student greatness; and coach masterfully for student greatness—and take our brilliant schools beyond the brink of greatness, to nurture and nourish the body, mind, and spirit that resides in every single human being in our classrooms, our schools, our gyms, our orchestras and science labs, our art rooms and playrooms. We must unlock the talent in our young people and offer them the empowerment of an independent mind, the freedom of an unbreakable spirit, and the serenity of an accomplished and giving human being.

References

Adolph, K. E., & Robinson, S. R. (2013). The road to walking: What learning to walk tells us about development. In P. D. Zelazo (Ed.), *Oxford handbook of developmental psychology* (Vol. 1, pp. 403–443). Retrieved from www.researchgate.net/publication/264047522_The_road_to_walking_What_learning_to_walk_tells_us_about_development

Anderson, M. (2016, June) *The modern educator—part one.* Retrieved from ictevangelist.com/the-modern-educator-part-one/

Assessment Training Institute. (2003). *Assessment for learning: A hopeful vision of the future* [Motion picture]. (Available from the Assessment Training Institute, Portland, OR)

Banks, D. (1997, February). The problem of excess genius. *Newsletter of the Classification Society of North America,* No. 48. Retrieved from groups.google.com/forum/#!topic/humanities.philosophy.objectivism/Et6esZjljt4

Barr, C. (2012, February 6). Deliberate practice: What it is and why you need it [Blog post]. Retrieved from expertenough.com/1423/deliberate-practice

Beechurst10. (2007, February 27). *Tiger Woods Nike golf commercial* [Video file]. Retrieved from www.youtube.com/watch?v=6oTMosZ76b8

Bellanca, J., Fogarty, R., & Pete, B. (2012). *How to teach thinking skills within the common core: 7 student proficiencies of the new national standards.* Bloomington IN: Solution Tree Press.

Black, P., & Wiliam, D. (1998). Inside the black box: Raising standards through classroom assessment. *Phi Delta Kappan, 80*(2), 139–148.

Blanchett, C. (2013). Cate Blanchett quotes. Retrieved from www.brainyquote.com/authors/cate_blanchett

Brookhart, S. M. (2008). *How to give effective feedback to your students.* Alexandria, VA: ASCD.

Butler, R. (1987). Task-involving and ego-involving properties of evaluation: Effects of different feedback conditions on motivational perceptions, interests, and performance. *Review of Educational Research, 65*(3), 245–281.

Butler, R. (1988). Enhancing and undermining intrinsic motivation; the effects of task-involving and ego-involving evaluation on interest and performance. *British Journal of Educational Psychology, 58,* 1–14.

Chappuis, J. (2009). *Seven strategies of assessment for learning.* Boston, MA: Pearson.

Chappuis, J., Stiggins, R., Chappuis, S., & Arter, J. A. (2012). *Classroom assessment for student learning: Doing it right—using it well* (2nd ed.). Boston, MA: Allyn & Bacon.

Chase, C. (2015, December 3). Lies! Tiger Woods never had Jack Nicklaus' 18 majors taped to wall. In *For the Win; USA Today*. Retrieved from ftw.usatoday.com/2015/12/tiger-woods-jack-nicklaus-majors-had-on-wall-never-did-goals-accomplishments-by-age

Chernow, R. (2004). *Alexander Hamilton*. New York, NY: Penguin.

Chernow, R. (2016). *Summary: Ron Chernow's Alexander Hamilton:* Ant Hive Media.

Cherry, K. (2016, October 3). What is the zone of proximal development? In *Verywell*. Retrieved from www.verywell.com/what-is-the-zone-of-proximal-development-2796034

Clymer, J. B., & Wiliam, D. (2007). Improving the way we grade science. *Educational Leadership, 64,* 36–42.

Colvin, G. (2008). *Talent is overrated: What really separates world-class performers from everybody else.* New York, NY: Portfolio.

Common Core State Standards. (2009). Development process. Retrieved from www.corestandards.org/about-the-standards/development-process/.

Common Core State Standards Initiative. (2010). *Preparing America's students for success.* Retrieved from www.corestandards.org/

Costa, A. L., & Kallick, B. (2009). *Learning and leading with habits of mind: 16 essential characteristics for success.* Alexandria, VA: ASCD.

Coyle, D. (2009). *The talent code: Greatness isn't born, it's grown, here's how.* New York, NY: Bantam Books.

Coyle, D. (2012). *The little book of talent: 52 tips for improving your skills.* New York, NY: Bantam.

Csikszentmihalyi, M. (2008). *Flow: The psychology of optimal experience.* New York, NY: Harper Perennial Modern Classics.

Danielson, C. (1996). *Enhancing professional practice: A framework for teaching.* Alexandria, VA: ASCD.

Deming, W. E. (1986). *Out of the crisis.* Cambridge, MA: MIT Press.

Duckworth, A. (2016). *Grit: The power of passion and perseverance.* London, United Kingdom: Vermilion.

Duckworth, S. (2016). *Sketchnotes for educators: 100 inspiring illustrations for lifelong learners.* Irvine, CA: EdTechTeam Press.

DuFour, R., & DuFour, R. (2012). *School leader's guide to professional learning communities at work.* Bloomington, IN: Solution Tree.

DuFour, R., DuFour, R., & Eaker, R. E. (2008). *Revisiting professional learning communities at work: New insights for improving schools.* Bloomington, IN: Solution Tree.

Duncan, C. (2016, May). The future of fact fluency. *BlueStreak Math.* Retrieved from www.bluestreakmath.com

Dweck, C. (2006). *Mindset: The new psychology of success.* New York, NY: Random House.

Dweck, C. S. (2007). The perils and promise of praise. *Educational Leadership, 65*(2), 34–39.

Dweck, C. S. (2016). *Mindset: The new psychology of success* (updated ed.). New York, NY: Random House.

Earl, L. M., & Timperley, H. (2014). Challenging conceptions of assessment.

In C. Wyatt-Smith, V. Klenowski, & P. Colbert (Eds.), *Designing assessment for quality learning: The enabling power of assessment* (Vol. 1, pp. 325–336). Dordrecht, Netherlands: Springer.

Edison, T. A. (n.d.). Thomas Alva Edison quotes. In *ThinkExist.com*. Retrieved from en.thinkexist.com/quotes/thomas_alva_edison/

Eichholz, T. (2016, May 16). 15 actionable strategies for increasing student motivation [Blog post]. Retrieved from www.gettingsmart.com/2016/08/15-actionable-strategies-for-increasing-student-motivation-and-engagement/amp/

Ericsson, K. A. (2012, October 28). The danger of delegating education to journalists: Why the APS observer needs peer review when summarizing new scientific developments [Blog post]. Retrieved from radical-scholarship.wordpress.com/2014/11/03/guest-post-the-danger-of-delegating-education-to-journalists-k-anders-ericsson/

Ericsson, K. A., & Charness, N. (1994). Expert performance: Its structure and acquisition. *American Psychologist, 49*(8), 725–747.

Ericsson, K. A., & Kintsch, W. (1995). Long-term working memory. *Psychological Review, 102*(2), 211–245.

Ericsson, K. A., Krampe, R. T., & Tesch-Römer, C. (1993). The role of deliberate practice in the acquisition of expert performance. *Psychological Review, 100*(3), 363–406.

Ericsson, K. A., & Pool, R. (2016a, April 10). Malcolm Gladwell got us wrong: Our research was key to the 10,000-hour rule, but here's what got oversimplified. Retrieved from www.salon.com/2016/04/10/malcolm_gladwell_got_us_wrong_our_research_was_key_to_the_10000_hour_rule_but_heres_what_got_oversimplified/

Ericsson, Karl A., & Pool, R. (2016b). *Peak: Secrets from the new science of expertise*. New York, NY: Houghton Mifflin.

Ericsson, K. A., Prietula, M. J., & Cokely, E. T. (2007). The making of an expert. *Harvard Business Review, 85*(7–8),114–121, 193. Retrieved from hbr.org/2007/07/the-making-of-an-expert

Fogarty, R. (1994). *How to teach for metacognitive reflection*. Palatine, IL: IRI/Skylight Training.

Fogarty, R., & Kerns, G. M. (2009). *Informative assessment: When it's not about a grade*. Thousand Oaks, CA: Corwin Press.

Fogarty, R., & Pete, B. M. (2017a). *Everyday problem-based learning: Quick projects to build problem-solving fluency*. Alexandria, VA: ASCD.

Fogarty, R., & Pete, B. M. (2017b). *From staff room to classroom: A guide for planning and coaching professional development* (2nd ed.). Thousand Oaks, CA: Corwin Press.

Folkard, S., & Monk, T. H. (1985). Circadian performance rhythms. In S. Folkard & T. H. Monk (Eds.), *Hours of work* (pp. 37–52). Chichester, United Kingdom: Wiley.

Fox, M. (2017). *Wilfrid Gordon McDonald Partridge* (J. Vivas, Illustrator). Gosford, NSW, Australia: Omnibus. (Original work published 1984)

Funston, S. (2005). *It's all in your head: A guide to your brilliant brain*. Toronto, Ontario: Maple Leaf.

Fusaro, M. (2008, May 29). What is teaching for understanding? [Blog post]. Retrieved from www.gse.harvard.edu/news/uk/08/05/what-teaching-understanding

Gallimore, R., & Tharp, R. (2004). What a coach can teach a teacher, 1975–2004: Reflections and re-analysis of John Wooden's teaching practices. *The Sport Psychologist, 18*(2), 119–137.

Galton, F. (2006). Hereditary genius: An inquiry into its laws and consequences. Amherst, NY: Prometheus Books. (Original work published 1869)

Gardner, H. (1999). *The disciplined mind: What all students should understand.* New York, NY: Simon & Schuster.

Giblin, G., Tor, E., & Parrington, L. (2016). The impact of technology on elite sports performance. *Sensoria: A Journal of Mind, Brain & Culture,12*(2), 3–9. Retrieved from www.researchgate.net/publication/311166052_The_impact_of_technology_on_elite_sports_performance

Gladwell, M. (2008). *Outliers: The story of success.* New York, NY: Back Bay Books and Little, Brown.

Green, E. (2015). *Building a better teacher: How teaching works (and how to teach it to everyone).* New York, NY: Norton.

Greulich, W. W. (1957). A comparison of the physical growth and development of American-born and native Japanese children. *American Journal of Physical Anthropology, 15*, 489–515.

Gruber, D. A. (2006). The craft of translation: An interview with Malcolm Gladwell. *Journal of Management Inquiry, 15*(4), 397–403. Retrieved from journals.sagepub.com/doi/abs/10.1177/1056492606294863

Guadagnoli, M., Holcomb, W., & Davis, M. (2002) The efficacy of video feedback for learning the golf swing. *Journal of Sports Sciences, 20*(8), 615–622. doi: 10.1080/026404102320183176

Hattie, J. (2012a). Feedback in schools. In R. Sutton, M. J. Hornsey, & K. Douglas (Eds.), *Feedback: The communication of praise, criticism, and advice* (pp. 265–278). New York, NY: Peter Lang.

Hattie, J. (2012b). *Visible learning: A synthesis of over 800 meta-analyses relating to achievement.* London, United Kingdom: Routledge.

The Hawn Foundation. (2003). MindUp: Our board of directors. Retrieved from mindup.org/thehawnfoundation/our-board-of-directors/

Hemingway, E. (1984). *Ernest Hemingway on writing* (L. W. Phillips, Ed.). New York, NY: Scribner.

Heritage, M. (2008). *Learning progressions: Supporting instruction and formative assessment.* Washington, DC: Council of Chief State School Officers. Retrieved from www.ccsso.org/Documents/2008/Learning_Progressions_Supporting_2008.pdf

Horwitz, A. (Director). (2016). *Hamilton's America* [video]. Retrieved from www.pbs.org/wnet/gperf/hamiltonfullfilm/5801/

Ice-cool Plyushchenko skates to top honours. (2006). International Olympic Committee. Retrieved from www.olympic.org/figure-skating

Jabr, F. (2011, December 8). Cache cab: Taxi drivers' brains grow to navigate London's streets. *Scientific American.* Retrieved from www.scientificamerican.com/article/london-taxi-memory/

Jackson, R. R. (2009). *Never work harder than your students and other principles of great teaching.* Alexandria, VA: Association for Supervision and Curriculum Development.

JustDisney.com. (1998, July 4). Walt Disney: a short biography. Retrieved from www.justdisney.com/walt_disney/biography/w_bio_short.html

Kamenetz, A. (2015, August 13). 5 big ideas that don't work in education. National Public Radio. Retrieved from www.npr.org/sections/ed/2015/08/13/430050765/five-big-ideas-that-don-t-work-in-education

Kamenetz, A. (2016, February 16). Standards, grades and tests are wildly outdated, argues "end of average." National Public Radio. Retrieved from www.npr.org/sections/ed/2016/02/16/465753501/standards-grades-and-tests-are-wildly-outdated-argues-end-of-average

Kirkup, C., Jones, E., Everett, H., Stacey, O., & Pope, E. (2014). *Developing national curriculum-based learning progressions: Mathematics.* Slough, United Kingdom: National Foundation for Educational Research.

Kluger, A. N., & DeNisi, A. (1996). The effects of feedback interventions on performance: A historical review, a meta-analysis, and a preliminary feedback intervention theory. *Psychological Bulletin, 119*(2), 254–284.

Kozol, J. (2007). *Letters to a young teacher.* New York, NY: Crown.

Laybourne, B. (2016, October 27). *Best trick shot this year* [Video file]. Retrieved from www.youtube.com/watch?v=vEGbVkDrwfg

Leahy, S., & Wiliam, D. (2011, April). *Devising learning progressions.* A paper presented at the annual meeting of the American Educational Research Association, New Orleans, LA.

Leahy, S., Lyon, C., Thompson, M., & Wiliam, D. (2005). Classroom assessment: Minute by minute, day by day. *Educational Leadership, 63*(3), 18–24.

Leder, M. (Director). (2000). *Pay it forward* [Motion picture]. United States: Warner.

Lemov, D., Woolway, E., & Yezzi, K. (2012). *Practice perfect: 42 rules for getting better at getting better.* San Francisco, CA: Jossey-Bass.

Libet, B. (1985, February 1). Unconscious cerebral initiative and the role of conscious will in voluntary action. *Behavioral and Brain Sciences, 8*(4), 529–539. Retrieved from Cambridge Core, www.cambridge.org/core/journals/behavioral-and-brain-sciences/article/unconscious-cerebral-initiative-and-the-role-of-conscious-will-in-voluntary-action/D215D2A77F-1140CD0D8DA6AB93DA5499

Magill, R. A., & Anderson, D. I. (2017). *Motor learning and control: Concepts and applications.* Dubuque, IA: McGraw-Hill Education.

Margolis, A. (2015, January 19). [No title.] In V. Strauss, Letting kids move in class isn't a break from learning: It *is* learning. *The Washington Post: Answer Sheet.* Retrieved from www.washingtonpost.com/news/answer-sheet/wp/2015/01/19/letting-kids-move-in-class-isnt-a-break-from-learning-it-is-learning/?utm_term=.312960e3cf3a

Molnar, M. (2016, January 23). Angela Duckworth tells educators: Grit + purpose = success. *Edweek Market Brief.* Retrieved from marketbrief.edweek.org/marketplace-k-12/12071/

Mosher, F. A. (2011). The role of learning progressions in standards-based education reform. *CPRE Policy Briefs.* Philadelphia, PA: University of

Pennsylvania, Graduate School of Education, Consortium for Policy Research in Education. Retrieved from repository.upenn.edu/cpre_policy-briefs/40

National Research Council. (2006). *Systems for state science assessment*. Washington, DC: The National Academies Press. doi.org/10.17226/11312

Palmer, T. (2015, June 20). 15 characteristics of a 21st-century teacher [Blog post]. Retrieved from www.edutopia.org/discussion/15-characteristics-21st-century-teacher

Park, A. (2016, August 13). Rio 2016 Olympics: Michael Phelps writes golden ending. *Time*. Retrieved from time.com/4451492/phelps-gold-medals-rio-2016-olympics-swimming-ledecky-simone-manuelgolden-finale-for-phelps-final-farewell/

Pellegrino, J. W. (2011). Building learning progressions. Paper presented at the Annual Meeting of the American Educational Research Association, New Orleans, LA.

Perdue, S. (1998) Sonny Perdue quotes. Retrieved from www.brainyquote.com/quotes/authors/sonny_perdue

Perkins, D. N. (2010). *Making learning whole: How seven principles of teaching can transform education*. San Francisco, CA: Jossey-Bass.

Pink, D. H. (2009). *Drive: The surprising truth about what motivates us*. New York, NY: Riverhead Books.

Pinker, S. (1997). *How the mind works*. New York, NY: Norton.

Popham, W. J. (2007). All about accountability/The lowdown on learning progressions. *Educational Leadership, 64*(7), 83–84. Retrieved from www.ascd.org/publications/educational-leadership/apr07/vol64/num07/The-Lowdown-on-Learning-Progressions.aspx

Popham, W. J. (2011, February 22). Formative assessment—A process, not a test. *Education Week*. Retrieved from www.edweek.org/ew/articles/2011/02/23/21popham.h30.html

Renaissance Learning. (2011). *A new, research-based approach to developing a learning progression for reading*. Wisconsin Rapids, WI: Renaissance Learning.

Ritchhart, R., Church, M., & Morrison, K. (2011). *Making thinking visible: How to promote engagement, understanding, and independence for all learners*. San Francisco, CA: Jossey-Bass.

Rose, T. (2015). *The end of average: How we succeed in a world that values sameness*. New York, NY: Penguin.

Rosen, J. (2014, November 10). The Knowledge, London's legendary taxi-driver test, puts up a fight in the age of GPS. *New York Times*. Retrieved from www.nytimes.com/2014/11/10/t-magazine/london-taxi-test-knowledge.html

Sadler, R. (2002). *Assessment in education: Principles, policy & practice*. Abingdon, United Kingdom: Carfax, 2002.

Schacter, J. (2000). Does individual tutoring produce optimal learning? *American Educational Research Journal, 37*(3), 801–829.

Shenk, D. (2011). *The genius in all of us: New insights into genetics, talent, and IQ*. New York, NY: Anchor Books.

Slavin, R. E. (1995). *Cooperative learning: Theory, research, and practice* (2nd ed.). Boston, MA: Allyn & Bacon.

Sockman, R.W. (n.d.) Ralph Sockman quotes. Retreived from www.brainyquote.

com/authors/ralph_w_sockman

Sood, A. (2013). *Mayo Clinic guide to stress-free living*. Philadelphia, PA: Da Capo Press.

Spencer, H. (1898). *The principles of biology*. Osnabrueck, Germany: Otto Zeller.

Spielberg, S. (2015). Steven Spielberg quotes. In *BrainyQuote*. Retrieved from www.brainyquote.com/quotes/authors/steven_spielberg

Stiggins, R. (2004). *Classroom assessment for student learning: Doing it right— using it well*. Portland, OR: Assessment Training Institute.

Stiggins, R. (2014). *Revolutionize assessment*. Thousand Oaks, CA: Corwin Press.

Swartz, R. J., & Perkins, D. N. (1990). *Teaching thinking: Issues and approaches*. Pacific Grove, CA: Midwest.

Syed, M. (2011). *Bounce: The myth of talent and the power of practice*. London, United Kingdom: HarperCollins.

Teaching the teachers. (2016, June 11). *The Economist*. Retrieved from www.economist.com/news/briefing/21700385-great-teaching-has-long-been-seen-innate-skill-reformers-are-showing-best

Tomlinson, C. A. (1999). *The differentiated classroom*. Alexandria, VA: ASCD.

Under Armour. (2014, September 10). *Misty Copeland: I will what I want* [Video]. Retrieved from www.youtube.com/watch?v=rtX91YGaBXw

University of the State of New York. (2011). *Common Core state standards for English language arts & literacy in history/social studies, science, and technical subjects*. Albany, NY: New York State Education Department.

Vygotsky, L. S. (1978). *Mind in society: The development of higher psychological processes* (M. Cole et al., Eds.). Cambridge, MA: Harvard University Press.

Vygotsky. L. (1986). *Thought and language*. Boston, MA: Massachusetts Institute of Technology.

Vygotsky (Vygotskij), L. S. (1996). *Thought and language* (A. Kozulin, Ed.). Cambridge, MA: MIT Press. (Original work published 1962)

Waack, S. (2015). Hattie effect size list: 195 influences related to achievement. *Visible Learning*. Retrieved from www.leg.state.nv.us/Session/79th2017/Exhibits/Assembly/ED/AED790I.pdf

Weir, P. (Director). (1989). *Dead poets society* [Motion picture]. United States: Touchstone Pictures.

Whitman, W. (1891). *Leaves of grass*. Philadelphia, PA: David McKay.

Wiliam, D. (2012). Every teacher can improve [video]. Retrieved from www.youtube.com/watch?v=eqRcpA5rYTE

Wiliam, D. (2011). *Embedded formative assessment*. Bloomington, IN: Solution Tree.

Wiliam, D. (2016). *Leadership for teacher learning: Creating a culture where all teachers improve so that all students succeed*. West Palm Beach, FL: Learning Sciences International.

Wiliam, D., & Leahy, S. (2015). *Embedding formative assessment: Practical techniques for K–12 classrooms*. West Palm Beach, FL: Learning Sciences International.

Williams, S. (2015). The ball is in your court. *Wired*. Retrieved from www.wired.com/2015/10/serena-williams-guest-editor-race-gender-equality/

Willis, J. (n.d.). Brain-based learning strategies: Hold students' attention with a radish. In *TeachHUB.com*. Retrieved from www.teachhub.com/brain-based-learning-strategies-hold-students-attention-radish

Willis, J. (2006). *Research-based strategies to ignite student learning: Insights from a neurologist and classroom teacher*. Alexandria, VA: ASCD. Retrieved from www.ascd.org/publications/books/107006.aspx

Willis, J. (2009). How to teach students about the brain. *Educational Leadership, 67*(4). Retrieved from www.ascd.org/publications/educational-leadership/dec09/vol67/num04/How-to-Teach-Students-About-the-Brain.aspx

Willis, J. (2010). *Learning to love math: Teaching strategies that change student attitudes and get results*. Alexandria, VA: ASCD.

Wilson, R. (2014, October 14). The profile of a modern teacher. In *Wayfaring Path* [Website].Retrieved from www.coetail.com/wayfaringpath/2014/10/14/the-profile-of-a-modern-teacher/

Wooden, J., & Jamison, S. (2005). *Wooden on leadership*. New York, NY: McGraw-Hill.

Wooden, J., & Tobin, J. (1972). *They call me coach*. Waco, TX: Word Books.

Index

About the Authors

Robin J. Fogarty is president of Robin Fogarty and Associates Ltd., a Florida-based, minority-owned, educational publishing/consulting company. Her doctorate is in curriculum and human resource development from Loyola University in Chicago. A leading proponent of the thoughtful classroom, Robin has trained educators throughout the world in curriculum, instruction, and assessment strategies. She has taught at all levels from kindergarten to college, served as an administrator, and consulted with state departments and ministries of education in the United States, Puerto Rico, Russia, Canada, Australia, New Zealand, Germany, Great Britain, Singapore, South Korea, and the Netherlands; her most recent work has been in the U.S. Virgin Islands, Bahrain, Dubai, and Abu Dhabi. Robin has published an impressive array of books, and her articles have appeared in *Educational Leadership, Phi Delta Kappan, The Journal of Staff Development, The Middle School Journal,* and *The Middle East Education Journal.*

Gene M. Kerns is a third-generation educator with teaching experience from elementary through the university level and K–12 administrative experience. He currently serves as vice president and chief academic officer of Renaissance Learning. With nearly 20 years of experience leading staff development and speaking at national and international conferences, his former clients include administrators' associations across the country, the Ministry of Education of Singapore, and London's Westminster Education Forum. His most recent work has been focused on assessment, new standards in both the United States and the United Kingdom, learning progressions, and personalized learning. Gene received his bachelor's degree and master's degree from Longwood College in Virginia, and also holds a doctor of education from the University of Delaware with an emphasis in education leadership.

Brian M. Pete is CEO and cofounder of Robin Fogarty & Associates, an international, educational consulting firm. A graduate of DePaul University in Chicago, he comes from a family of educators that includes college professors, school superintendents, teachers, and teachers of teachers. Brian has a rich background in professional development and is entering his 17th year as an author/presenter working exclusively with the adult learner. Brian visits schools throughout the United States, Europe, and Asia, including the U.S. Virgin Islands, Australia, New Zealand, Singapore, and the United Arab Emirates. He has an eye for the "teachable moment" and the words to describe what he sees as skillful teaching. Brian is coauthor of the award-winning book *The Right to Be Literate* and has just completed a 2nd edition of *Staff Room I*. Currently he is designing an online course for high school students to foster mindfulness and decisionmaking, as well as a new book, *Everyday PBL: Developing Problem Solving Fluency*.